Contents

Egyptian Life

Miriam Stead

Published for
the Trustees of the British Museum by
British Museum Publications

932 STE

© 1986 The Trustees of the British Museum

Published by British Museum Publications Ltd
46 Bloomsbury Street, London WC1B 3QQ

Third impression 1989

ISBN 0-7141-2040-5

Designed by Roger Davies

Printed in Italy by New Interlitho, Milan

Front cover Middle Kingdom tomb model of a peasant ploughing with a pair of oxen. Length 43 cm (no. 52947).

Inside front cover Ancient Egyptian furniture (see fig. 18).

Title page Plucking grapes, from the tomb of Khaemwese at Thebes (detail of fig. 41).

This page A village on the banks of the Nile. The mud-brick houses are similar in many ways to their ancient counterparts and, as in antiquity, trees are grown to provide fruit and shade.

Inside back cover Ducks and fish in a garden pool (detail of fig. 13).

Back cover Wooden figure of a serving girl carrying on her head a basket of loaves and joints of meat. Middle Kingdom, *c.* 1900 BC. Height 39 cm (no. 30716).

THE TRUSTEES OF THE BRITISH MUSEUM acknowledge with gratitude the generosity of **THE HENRY MOORE FOUNDATION** for the grant which made possible the publication of this book

1 The Home

The population of ancient Egypt was divided between a number of towns which grew up at regular intervals along the Nile and innumerable small villages which clustered around the facilities offered by these urban centres. Most important were the royal cities, chosen by the Pharaohs as their chief seats and centres of the nation's government. Throughout the course of Egyptian history a number of places held this honour, such as Memphis, Thebes, Itjtowy, El-Amarna, Pi-Ramesse and later Tanis, Bubastis, Sais and, under the Ptolemies, Alexandria. Next in importance were the nome capitals, which acted as centres for local administration and taxation, as well as housing the temples of the major regional deities. Then there were towns of some importance which lacked the political status of nome capitals, such as Abydos, famous as a centre of pilgrimage to the shrine of the god Osiris.

Many towns and villages had a long history of occupation, indeed a good number of ancient sites are inhabited to this day. One of the reasons for this long-term habitation of certain locations was the annual rise of the Nile which, until the 1960s, inundated the whole valley of Egypt. To escape the waters, dwellings had to be built either in the desert margins or on the limited amount of elevated ground within the areas of cultivation. Also, the means by which ancient Egyptian buildings were constructed meant that over the centuries the height of the inhabited mounds grew, making them even safer from the flood. For everything, from palaces and administrative buildings to houses and, until the New Kingdom, even temples, was constructed of unbaked mud-brick. Even in the dry Egyptian climate such a fragile material is fairly short-lived, and as the structures decayed, the inhabitants merely demolished them and built on the remains and on the uncleared heaps of rubbish that surrounded them. As time passed, villages and towns rose above the surrounding countryside, forming quite considerable hills, now called *tells*. This phenomenon is common throughout the Near East. Unfortunately, where occupation has ceased the majority of these *tells* have been denuded by peasant farmers, who find the decayed mud-brick an excellent fertiliser. This has reduced the quantity of ancient dwelling sites available for excavation, and the number is even further reduced because, as has already been mentioned, many ancient towns and villages are still under occupation. Nevertheless, there is still a substantial amount of archaeological evidence available, which supplies ground plans of ancient houses and some idea of their decoration and setting. To these bare bones can be added information from artistic and documentary sources, as well as objects found in tombs, which help us to visualise a complete dwelling.

The majority of Egyptian towns and villages seem to have developed in a piecemeal, haphazard fashion around a central core of public buildings. Town planning did exist, but, as we shall see, it was limited to specialised types of community created for specific, official purposes. There is also evidence of planning in the central government and palace quarters of the major cities, notably El-Amarna, which has been extensively excavated.

The organic growth of residential areas in large towns and small villages can be illustrated both archaeologically and from documentary papyri. A village of the late New Kingdom has been excavated within the walls of the mortuary temple of Ramesses III at Medinet Habu. It consists of modest homes, 2 which, according to the excavators, were laid out arbitrarily and without planning. Separating the houses are narrow alleyways which wander crookedly up and downhill, with steps to negotiate the rubbish heaps on which the village is partly built. Groups of houses are constructed around central courts or blind al-

1 Mud-brick is still used as a building material for houses in Egypt and is made in the same way as in antiquity. Chopped straw is mixed with Nile mud and the bricks shaped in a wooden mould. They are then left to dry in the sun.

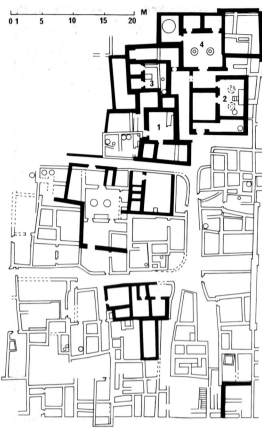

the development of a single property by a large family can be followed in a group of legal documents from Thebes. In 343 BC the owner of the house, Djufachi, a carpenter, divided it between five members of his family. Over the next forty years ownership of the divided property passed to other members of the family and to others connected to it by marriage. Eventually, through foreclosure and sale, the properties moved outside the extended family group, but by then the form of the original house had altered and grown into an organic series of dwellings.

Even within the planned residential zones of El-Amarna a similar pattern can be discerned. Groups of small houses cluster around courtyards, often with shared facilities. These clumps of modest homes tend to be grouped round the mansions of the rich, and their inhabitants were probably the retainers and dependants of the great men.

In marked contrast to these homely, organic settlements are planned, organised communities. Into this category fall the towns built for the workmen who constructed the pyramids

2 (*left*) Part of the New Kingdom village at Medinet Habu. Houses 1–4 show how housing developed to meet the needs of succeeding generations: 1 and 2 are accessible from the street, while 3 and 4 can only be entered through a gate into a private alley. The antechamber of house 4 is connected with house 2 and may represent an extension of it or a separate property acquired and modified for a growing family.

3 Part of a residential area of El-Amarna, showing the small houses of dependants grouped around the mansions of the rich. Even in this new city, built on a fresh site where there was plenty of space, the dwellings of the poor clustered together and developed in the same organic way as in unplanned towns and villages.

leyways, some of which are closed off from the street by gateways. It is evident that houses within these small complexes gradually altered and grew to meet the needs of succeeding generations of occupants. Occupation of housing by extended family groups can also be demonstrated by documentary papyri from several periods of Egyptian history. For instance, the household of Hekanakhte, a mortuary priest of the Twelfth Dynasty from the village of Nebeseyet near Thebes, consisted of his mother, his concubine, a female dependent relative, five men who may have been his sons, three women probably his daughters, the agent of the estate and his family, and finally a number of servants.

Approximately seventeen centuries later,

and later inhabited by the priests who maintained the funerary cult of the deceased Pharaoh, the fortress towns of Nubia, and villages built for those engaged in the excavation and decoration of New Kingdom royal tombs, such as at Deir el-Medina and El-Amarna. These communities possessed certain common characteristics. They were usually in inhospitable, remote areas, without their own water supply, and were surrounded by rectangular or sub-rectangular walls, within which the streets and houses were laid out in a regular pattern, either in straight rows or a grid. Individual dwellings were of uniform size and design, except for one or two larger houses inhabited by the foreman or administrators.

4 The workmen's village at El-Amarna was a poor, unpleasant place consisting of seventy-two housing units plus a larger overseer's dwelling. The houses were small and cramped, measuring approximately five by ten metres. The narrow streets were cluttered with water jars and tethering posts for animals, and animals seem also to have been sheltered in the entrance rooms of the dwellings. Beyond the entrance was the main living and sleeping room, which was divided into two tiny chambers, one a kitchen, the other a second bedroom or store. In the kitchen area was a stairway to the roof.

The village of Deir el-Medina, although similar in concept, was far more prosperous and the individual houses were somewhat larger – about five by fifteen metres – and better appointed, especially later in its history.

5 The original Eighteenth Dynasty settlement was sub-rectangular in shape and consisted of one street, off which the workmen's dwellings opened. Unlike El-Amarna, which only survived a few years, Deir el-Medina existed for over four centuries and during that time interesting developments took place. The community expanded until there were seventy units within the walls and about fifty outside. The

6, 7

main street was lengthened, but it developed a dog-leg and new subsidiary alleyways appeared. The interiors of the houses were modified or amalgamated to suit the needs of individual families, and rooms were converted for private enterprise into shops, workshops and bars. In short, it came to resemble the normal, haphazard kind of Egyptian village.

Instead of being used as a stable, the entrance room of a typical house at Deir el-Medina was set up as a household chapel with niches for offerings, stelae and busts. On the wall was painted an image of the god Bes, one of the family deities associated with childbirth, and a brick construction found in these

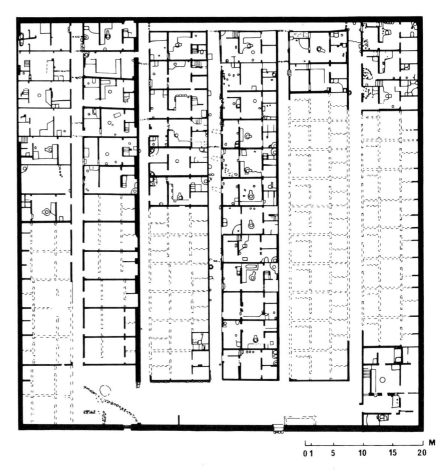

M
0 1   5   10   15   20

4 The workmen's village at El-Amarna consisted of rows of mean, barrack-like dwellings where animals lived as well as people. Many houses had keyhole-shaped hearths and storage jars sunk into the floor. There was no well in the village and water had to be brought from some distance away.

5 The first phase of the workmen's village at Deir el-Medina, in the Eighteenth Dynasty. Two contiguous rows of ten basic houses stand on each side of a central alleyway.

6 Deir el-Medina in the Nineteenth and Twentieth Dynasties. The village has almost doubled in size since its foundation and the houses have been modified and embellished. Like its counterpart at El-Amarna, this workmen's village lacked its own water supply. Water was carried to the site and stored in a guarded tank outside the main gate.

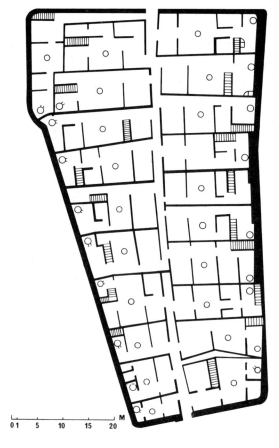

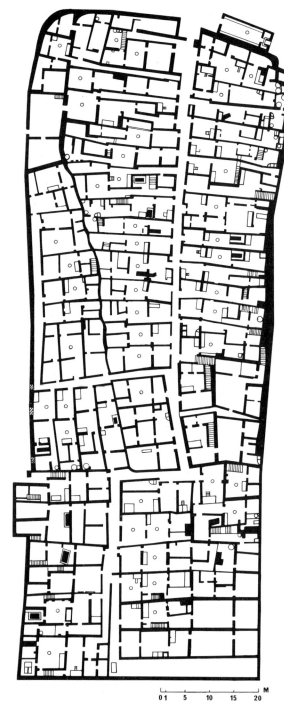

chapels may have served as a birthing bed.

8 The antechamber led into the main room of the house, the ceiling of which was quite lofty and supported by one or more columns. Against one wall was a raised dais, plastered and whitewashed, which served as an eating area by day and a bed at night. Beneath this platform was often a cellar. Leading from this principal room were one or two small chambers for sleeping or storage. At the rear of the house was a small walled court which served as the kitchen. Here there was an oven, a grain silo and grinding equipment. In some houses there was another cellar sunk beneath the yard. The roof of the house was reached by a staircase ascending from the kitchen court.

How does this compare with the houses in less organised settlements? In both Medinet Habu and the main city at El-Amarna, the one- or two-roomed houses of the very poor are interspersed with the larger four- to six-room dwellings of the artisan class. The basic house type at El-Amarna was square or almost square in plan. The main feature was a central living room, its roof supported by one or more columns and with a dais to one side. This room was preceded by an antechamber and entrance loggia. Ranged around this main chamber were the bedrooms, women's quarters and storerooms. This form applied to houses of all classes, differences in status being reflected in the size and number of the rooms and the quality of materials used. Cooking facilities were outside the main dwelling, either in outbuildings or in communal courtyards. Many houses had staircases to the roof, or perhaps a second storey.

Of especial interest at Amarna is the evidence for sanitary arrangements. Many houses had a suite consisting of a bathroom and lavatory leading from one of the major bedrooms. The bathroom was formed of a low screen wall sheathed in limestone. The bather stood on another slab of stone and poured water over himself or had water poured over him. The excess ran out to a vessel which could be removed and emptied. The lavatory was a seat set above a large vessel containing sand. In the many ancient Egyptian houses that no doubt lacked such sophisticated arrangements, portable commode stools may have been used, again placed over a sand-filled vessel.

Turning to the remains of Medinet Habu, we find the plan of the houses basically similar to those at Amarna: square or almost square with an antechamber leading into the main living room with columns and dais. Although it is perhaps dangerous to generalise from so few examples, it is not unreasonable to

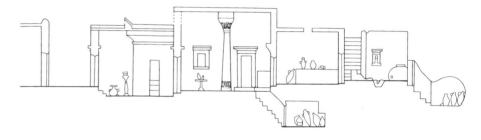

suppose that this 'villa' type of housing was common in unplanned Egyptian settlements.

There is, however, one interesting example which points to another type of housing which may have existed in the residential districts of old, established cities such as Thebes. This is found in a scene from the tomb of Djehuty- 9 nefer at Thebes and shows a multi-storey type of 'town house'.

The right-hand part of the scene is missing. This may have shown the main door and entrance loggia of the house. Above where the entrance should be are the fragmentary remains of two rooms with servants at work. These may be the bedrooms, or possibly servants' quarters or workrooms. A staircase runs

7 (*top*) The ruins of the workmen's village of Deir el-Medina. The enclosure wall and main street are clearly visible.

8 A typical house at Deir el-Medina, with three main rooms and a yard which acted as a kitchen. There were often two cellars for storage. The niches set into the walls contained religious stelae, images of household gods and family ancestors.

The doorway into this chamber is elaborately decorated with a lattice-work pattern. The roof of the chamber is characteristically high and the rafters are decorated in a block design. The columns supporting the roof are also decorated and all these features would have been brightly painted. The living room is lit by clerestory windows near the ceiling.

On the top floor of the house Djehuty-nefer is shown working in his office. Servants carry produce into his presence to be inspected and recorded by scribes. The bearers have to ascend a short flight of steps to enter the office. Its height above the other rooms on this floor is a result of its position above the living room, which is taller than the other rooms of the house. This added height carries on to the roof and a flight of steps can be seen leading to a group of five storage bins.

An impression of the exterior of such a 'town house' may be gained from a limestone model. This depicts a tall, thin house, with a 10 narrow doorway raised above ground level. Windows set at different levels indicate the floors. The lower set have simple cross bars, the upper ones are latticed. The tops of the walls form a parapet around the roof, creating a courtyard. The brickwork or decorated plaster is shown by horizontal bands running round the building and the small rectangles which appear in courses may be timber supports. Another, much simpler, house model reveals a common type of doorway found in ancient Egyptian houses, which imitates the entrance to a temple. The jambs and lintels 12 would probably have been made of wood covered with plaster and in this case they are painted with red and black stripes. Set into the side wall of the model are two windows and on 11 the roof is a small court with a shelter to one side.

Not all Egyptians lived in cramped urban or village conditions. On the outskirts of towns and in the open countryside there was room

9 The 'town house' of Djehuty-nefer, from his tomb at Thebes. In the absence of archaeological evidence for housing in the heart of ancient Thebes, it is impossible to say whether this type of dwelling was common there. Nevertheless, the painting is of particular interest for the information it gives about the internal arrangements of an Egyptian home.

the full height of the house and further servants are shown carrying food and vessels up to the roof. At the top of the staircase is a canopied area which could well be a kitchen, for a servant is shown preparing food and to locate the kitchen on the open roof would ensure that cooking smells were carried away over the rooftops. Also on the roof are a number of storage bins and grain silos.

The basement of the house is given over to other domestic activities such as spinning and weaving, the grinding of corn and sieving of grain. The ceiling is supported by very solid, but plain, columns. The first floor of the house contains the main apartments. Servants are shown carrying food through an antechamber to their master, Djehuty-nefer, who is seated on a chair placed on the ubiquitous dais. Servants proffer him flowers and food.

10 Although highly schematic, these limestone models give an impression of the exterior of an Egyptian house. Height 21 cm and 14 cm (nos 2462 and 27526).

11 (*below left*) Latticed window-grille from a house at El-Amarna. It is painted brown, probably to reduce glare. Height 43.5 cm (no. 63517).

12 Gaily painted plaster fragment from the exterior of a house at El-Amarna. It was probably part of the decoration above the principal doorway, as seen in the house model in fig. 10. Height 38 cm (no. 58846).

for more expansive building. Indeed it seems to have been the dream of most urban dwellers to escape into these more pleasant surroundings. Some of the country estates shown in tomb paintings, therefore, represent an ideal aspired to for the afterlife rather than a property which the tomb-owner possessed during his lifetime. This wish for an idyllic rural retreat is also expressed in writing, for example in this description by Ra'ia, the chief overseer of the cattle of the god Amun:

Ra'ia has built a goodly villa which is opposite Edjo. He built it on the verge (of the river) as a work of eternity and planted trees on every side of it. A channel is dug in front of it, and sleep is broken (only) by the splash of the wave. One does not become tired at the sight of it; one is gay at its portal and drunk in its hall. Fine doorposts hewn anew, and walls inlaid with lapis lazuli. Its granaries are supplied with plenty and packed (?) with abundance; a fowl-yard and an aviary with *ro*-geese; byres full of oxen; a breeding pond with geese; horses in the stable; (boats) are moored at its quay. The poor, old and young, come to live in its neighbourhood. Your sustenance is assured . . . Joy dwells within it.

The architectural reality of this type of villa estate can be found in the great mansions of El-Amarna, even if here the setting is less idyllic. The great villas lie at the heart of estates surrounded by mud-brick enclosure walls. Around each house are a number of outbuildings: servants' quarters, including a house for the steward, kitchens, stables, workrooms, storerooms and a number of circular granaries. The purpose of these was probably to store the grain which was paid as subsistence to the dependants who lived outside the walls of the estate.

A major feature of the Amarna walled mansions is the open space which formed the garden. Gardens were the delight of the ancient Egyptians. There they grew multitudes of brilliant flowers and trees for shade and nurtured

fruits and vegetables which required constant watering. A central feature of these gardens were pools, which were both decorative and provided the water for irrigation. The remains of such pools, or possibly wells, are shown as dotted lines on the plan of Amarna houses. Wells are in fact more likely in this case as the city was built beyond the limit of cultivation and the water table was too deep for pools to be viable.

A house complete with its garden is depicted in the *Book of the Dead* of Nakhte, a royal scribe of the Eighteenth Dynasty. Nakhte and his wife are shown standing in front of their house, before which are planted a fruit tree and a date palm for ornament and shade. The form of the house is greatly simplified but shows several interesting features. The walls are whitewashed to reflect the heat, like those

13 Garden with a decorative pool, which would also have been used to water the trees and plants. Gardens served the dual purpose of providing ornament and a shady retreat and nurturing fruit trees and vegetables, which required constant irrigation. Height 64 cm (no. 37983).

14 (*opposite, above*) Middle Kingdom 'soul house', with a rounded doorway and one decorated window. A staircase leads up to the roof, where the family would have lived in hot weather. On the roof is a vent to catch cool breezes and a spout to drain off water. Height 17.3 cm (no. 32610).

of many houses in Egypt today. The elaborate doorway is coloured reddish-brown, as are the windows, probably indicating that they were made of wood. The lattice windows are shown high up on the wall and may be clerestory windows for the main room. On the roof are two triangular vents. These were designed to catch the cooling breezes, greatly desired and prayed for by the ancient Egyptians.

An idea of a more humble rural home may be gained from a series of models placed in tombs during the Middle Kingdom, known as 'soul houses'. These are crude clay models of 14 modest homesteads standing in small enclosures. The forecourt of the house acts as an offering tray and on it are modelled food-offerings for the deceased. The models are very schematic, but give some impression of the type of dwelling inhabited by a poor farmer.

15 (*below*) House and garden of the scribe Nakhte. The house is built on a platform to prevent damp rising into the mud-brick walls and to raise it above possible flooding (no. 10471, sheet 21).

To complete this picture of the ancient Egyptian home it remains to consider the decorations and furnishings with which the Egyptians surrounded themselves. The interior walls of their houses were often painted in bright colours or decorated with patterns and scenes, often with floral or vegetal motifs. Representations of gods were also used, especially household deities, who brought good luck to the inhabitants. Walls left plain were usually whitewashed.

The ancient Egyptians had a limited range of furnishings, and these were simple in design although the standard of craftsmanship could be high. Individual pieces were often painted in bright colours or veneered with high-quality wood. Inlaid decoration was also common, using glass, stones and faience, although the finest pieces were inlaid with ebony and ivory.

The most common article of furniture was 17 the stool, used by all Egyptians including Pharaoh. Among the numerous varieties were a low stool only a few centimetres high, with a rush seat; an animal-legged stool; an elaborately decorated stool with flared legs and a leather seat; a folding stool with legs often terminating in ducks' heads, and a lattice-work stool with elaborate bracing. Chairs also existed, but they were far rarer than stools and by and large they denoted the high social status of the owner. The most usual type of chair had animal-shaped legs and a slanted back-rest. Another variety was low and very wide with a straight back, while a third is reminiscent of a posture chair designed at the Bauhaus. Tables were also widely used and came in a variety of forms from simple constructions of wickerwork to elaborate wooden designs with lattice supports. They were all small and low and would have been used by one or two people at most when dining.

The ancient Egyptians slept comfortably in well-made wooden beds, which consisted of a 18 wooden framework standing on animal-shaped legs and a woven rush support for the body. At one end was a footboard, often decorated. Instead of pillows the Egyptians used headrests, consisting of a curved neckpiece set on top of a pillar which sat on an oblong base. They were mostly made of wood, although some are of stone. A few examples have been found wrapped in several layers of cloth to mitigate their hardness. Bed coverings were made of linen and stored, when not in use, in chests of wood or woven reed. Chests were used to store all manner of domestic possessions in the same way as we use cupboards and chests of drawers today. Some were plain and others decorated with painted patterns and inlay.

In the evenings lamps were lit during the brief interlude following the evening meal before the household went early to bed, to rise again at dawn. These were for the most part simple bowls of pottery or stone containing oil and a wick. They could be placed on the floor or higher up in wall niches. Examples of lamp 16 stands have been found, consisting of a column, sometimes in papyrus form, on top of which are three pegs supporting a bowl which forms the lamp proper. Pottery torches are also known; these were set in brackets on the wall.

An indication of the amount of furniture and other possessions owned by members of the artisan class is given by ostraca found at Deir el-Medina, one of which is an inventory of items left in a house there by Pashed and his wife Sheritre: 3 sacks of barley, 1½ sacks of emmer corn, 26 bunches of onions, 2 beds, 1 chest, 2 *krt* for a man, 2 folding stools, 1 clothes chest, 1 large filled chest, 2 bases for cooking stoves, 1 bottom (?), 2 foot stools, 2 wooden folding stools, 1¾ sacks of beans, 12 blocks of natron, 2 wooden *igr*, 1 door, 2 sawn *strt*, 2 wooden serving trays, 1 small woven serving tray, 1 stone pestle, 2 wooden *md3y*.

16 (*left*) Wooden lamp stand in the form of a papyrus column, with the remains of painted decoration. On top of the stand are three pegs to support a lamp. (The lamp shown here does not belong with the stand.) Height 89 cm (nos 35763 and 27440).

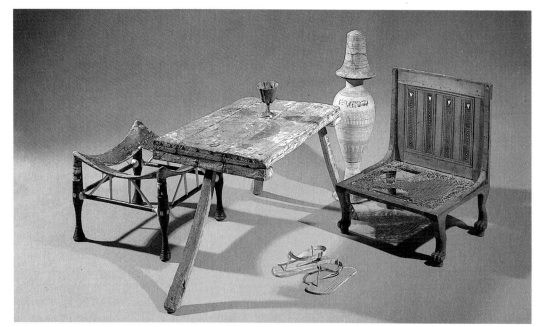

17 Ancient Egyptian furniture, including a three-legged table, an ornate stool with flared legs, and a low, wide chair with fine inlay of ebony and ivory. Behind the table is a decorated wine-jar from El-Amarna.

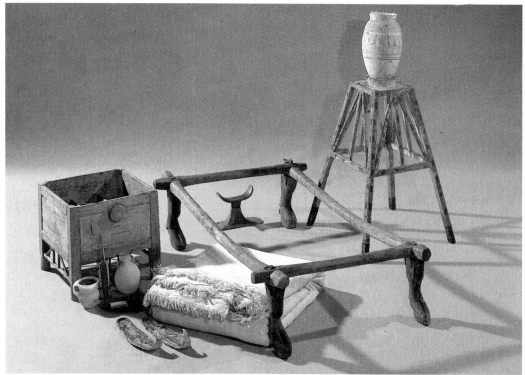

18 A bed-frame with animal legs, a head-rest, a linen sheet and a pot-stand. The cosmetic chest of the lady Tutu, wife of the scribe Ani, stands beside the bed.

2 The Family and Society

The founding and continuation of a family line was important in ancient Egyptian society and early marriage was encouraged. 'Take a wife while you are young, that she may make a son for you. She should bear for you while you are youthful. It is proper to create people. Happy the man whose people are many, he is saluted on account of his offspring' (*Instructions of Ani*). A suitable age for a man to marry was twenty, according to the teachings of the scribe Onkhsheshonqy, and his bride would be even younger. The stele of the lady Tjaiemhotep indicates that she was only fourteen years old when she married a future high priest of Ptah at Memphis in the first century BC.

Marriages tended to be within the same social group and even within the same family, although rarely between brother and sister as once used to be thought, at least until the Ptolemaic period. The words 'brother' and 'sister' found in legal documents and literature were often used simply as terms of endearment. The most common family marriages were between uncle and niece or cousins.

No doubt many marriages were arranged and parental consent was certainly needed, but the highly romantic tone of Egyptian love poetry indicates that young people had fairly wide latitude in bestowing their affections: 'My brother torments my heart with his voice, he makes sickness take hold of me; he is neighbour to my mother's house, and I cannot go to him! Brother, I am promised to you by the Gold of Women (Hathor)! Come to me that I may see your beauty.'

Once a marriage had been agreed, a contract was drawn up to establish the rights of both parties to maintenance and possessions. The notable and interesting point about these documents is the equality of women with men in their ability to own, manage and receive property. If a marriage ended in divorce the rights of the wife were equally protected. She was entitled to support from her husband, especially if she was repudiated by him through no fault of her own. The amount she received might equal her third of the marriage settlement, or perhaps even more. If the woman was divorced through her own guilt, usually of adultery, she still had certain rights to maintenance from her former husband.

The marriage process seems to have been simple. One partner, usually the bride, moved into the household of the other; no religious or civil ceremony was required. The marriage settlement amounted only to a private legal agreement. It seems likely, however, that there were family parties and festivities to celebrate a wedding. Divorce was equally easy. One party simply repudiated the other, with or without their consent, and then one of them, again usually the wife, removed herself from the conjugal home. Nevertheless, the financial impositions placed on the husband consequent to a divorce meant that he could not rid himself of his wife without some thought.

This, to us, apparently casual attitude did

19 (*below*) Marriage contract between Pagosh, a priest, and Teteimhotep, in which he agrees to pay her a stipulated amount of money within thirty days in the event of their divorce. The contract dates from 172 BC. Width 51 cm (no. 10593).

20 (*right*) An unknown couple from Thebes, their hands clasped in a gesture of marital affection. New Kingdom, c. 1350 BC. Height 132 cm (no. 36).

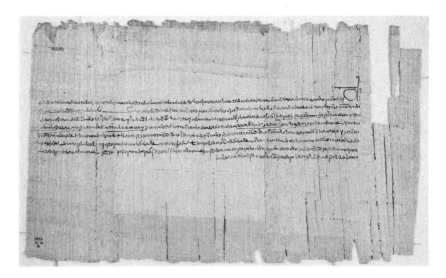

not mean that Egyptian marriages were necessarily short-lived or lacking in affection. The passage of love poetry quoted above indicates the degree of youthful passion before marriage and ancient Egyptian wisdom literature demonstrates the respect due to a wife:

Do not control your wife in her house when you know she is efficient. Do not say to her 'Where is it?, Get it!', when she has put it in the right place. Let your eye observe in silence. Then you recognise her skill, it is joy when your hand is with her, there are many who do not understand this. If a man desists from strife at home, he will not meet its beginning. Every man who founds a household should hold back the hasty heart. (*Instructions of Ani*)

Many statues and wall paintings show married couples clasping each other in obvious 20 gestures of affection. Occasionally we find a personal testament of the love of a husband for his wife. For example, a papyrus now in Leiden contains a letter from a distraught widower to his deceased wife. The pair had married young but as the anonymous writer rose high in Pharaoh's service he had refused to put aside his wife, who was presumably low-born. The unspoken implication is that many other men in his position would have done so. Instead, he had always honoured and cared for her. When she had fallen sick the best physicians had been consulted, and while travelling with the king during her illness, he had not eaten properly for worry, rushing home to her side as soon as Pharaoh returned to Memphis. In the three years since she had died, he had lived alone and not sought company, especially that of women, although it was expected of a man in his position.

The answer to this grief-stricken invocation might be found in the stele of Tjaiemhotep already mentioned. In a final address she exhorts her husband: 'Cease not to drink, to eat, to get drunk, to enjoy making love, to make the day joyful, to follow your inclination day

21 Magical amulet from the New Kingdom in the form of a woman lying on a bed with a baby by her side. Its purpose was to ensure a safe and easy birth. Length 23.5 cm (no. 2371).

and night, do not allow grief to enter your heart.'

On the other hand, there are frequent references in Egyptian literature which suggest that women, especially unattached women, were objects of some suspicion, ready to entrap the unwary male. The *Instructions of Ani* warn: 'Beware of a strange woman [i.e. a prostitute], one not known in her town. Do not stare at her when she goes by, do not make love to her. A deep water whose course is unknown, such is a woman away from her husband.' Similarly, the *Instructions of Ptahhotep* warn against approaching a woman in another man's house: the penalty for dalliance is likely to be death.

A whole catalogue of pithy comments on the shortcomings of the fair sex is to be found in the *Instructions of Onkhsheshonqy*, although it is to be hoped that they are tongue-in-cheek: 'Instructing a woman is like having a sack of sand whose side is split open!'; 'let your wife see your wealth, do not trust her with it!'; 'do not open your heart to your wife, what you have said to her goes into the street!'.

The chief object of marriage was to have children, especially a son, not only to continue the family line but also to provide a proper burial for his parents and to ensure that the correct rituals were carried out for their spirits. If a couple were childless they appealed to the gods, as in the *Tale of the Doomed Prince* in which the king, without an heir, 'begged a son for himself from the gods of his domain and they decreed one should be born to him'. The main deities concerned with fertility and child-bearing were Hathor and Taweret, although in the Late Period Imhotep, the god of medicine, was also invoked.

Egyptian women gave birth crouching or kneeling on two to four bricks, placed apart to allow the child to be disengaged from the mother, who was usually attended by at least two midwives. A description of a birth can be found in the *Tales of Wonder* contained in the

22

24

22 (*far left*) The goddess Taweret, shown as an upright, pregnant hippopotamus, was especially associated with childbirth. Prayers were offered to her for a safe delivery, and a large number of amulets and votive figures depicting her survive from the Late Period. Height 17 cm (no. 11862).

23 Anthropomorphic vase showing a woman breast-feeding a baby. It may have been used to contain mother's milk as a medicine for a sick child. Height 14 cm (no. 24653).

Westcar Papyrus. A woman named Ruddedit gives birth to three future rulers of Egypt, after which she undergoes 'a cleansing of fourteen days'. This presumably consisted of a period of rest and care to avoid post-natal infections, which would have been hard to cure. Some remedies to combat such problems are given in medical papyri, but the prescriptions are unlikely to have had much practical effect.

Once born, the child was breast-fed by the mother for the first three years of its life. A series of anthropomorphic vases depict

23 women breast-feeding babies and these may have been used to contain mother's milk as a

24 Part of an inscription from a temple wall or a trial piece showing a woman giving birth, kneeling on two bricks. This stylised representation forms the hieroglyph denoting childbearing. Height 18.1 cm (no. 61062).

medicine for sick children, although again such a remedy contained a stronger element of suggestive magic than genuine help.

At birth the child was given a name by its mother. The choice of name was motivated by one of several factors. Some names reflect the immediate circumstances of the birth or perhaps the divine intervention which brought it about. Others indicate the power or popularity of a god at a particular time, or perhaps the local deity of a town or village. Names including that of the ruling Pharaoh or dynasty are also frequent, as are those which fit a person into his or her family tree, especially among royal, noble or priestly houses. Many Egyptian names were long and not suited to social usage, and many people therefore acquired a nickname, given by family or friends but also used in legal documents.

The period of childhood before education, apprenticeship and work was short, but not totally non-existent. Various toys have survived, such as balls, tops, dolls and figures of animals with moving parts, not dissimilar to wooden playthings given to children today. There are also depictions of boys and girls engaged in group activities such as athletic games, mock battles with sticks and gymnastic dancing. Other sporting activities which were encouraged, at least among the royal family and nobility, were swimming, archery and horsemanship.

Education in Egypt was largely vocational, an apprenticeship served within the family trade or craft, usually under the boy's father. We know something of the system from the craftsmen's community of Deir el-Medina. Boys were taught skills by their father in the hope of at least one son winning a place in the official corps of tomb-builders. Those youths who were most likely to be accepted were designated 'children of the tomb'. They were attached to one of the gangs to do odd jobs and run messages, but no doubt primarily to

25 The head of a young prince. He wears a short wig and the 'lock of youth', a plait of hair which was allowed to grow over the right side of children's faces in ancient Egypt. Nineteenth Dynasty, c. 1340 BC. Height 26 cm (no. 68682).

watch and learn until such time as a place became available for them. Offspring who failed to achieve one of these coveted, lucrative positions had to leave the village, either to set up as craftsmen elsewhere or to seek a different type of job.

A more formal, academic education was reserved for those who trained to be scribes. Elementary schooling for these privileged children, mostly boys, began at about five years of age and consisted of repeated recitation of lessons as well as the copying of standard texts. The basic primer may have been a book called *Kemyt*, which means 'completion'. The form and style of the surviving copies of this work indicate that it was composed in the Middle Kingdom, although it was still used a thousand years later. The reason for its continued popularity as a teaching book was the simplicity of its language and the fact that the text was set out in vertical columns rather than horizontal lines, so that the signs were easier for young children to copy. The contents of the *Kemyt* consisted of model letters, phrases and expressions useful to scribes, plus

26, 27

26 The scribe Pes-shu-per, shown with an unrolled papyrus on his lap. Scribes were the educated élite of Egyptian society and looked down with contempt on other men. Twenty-fifth Dynasty, c.750 BC. Height 53 cm (no. 1514).

85

assorted wisdom texts giving advice to would-be scholars.

Having mastered the basics, the student could progress to more advanced texts. The majority of these were classics of Egyptian literature, in particular the wisdom texts full of pronouncements on morals and behaviour for young men who hoped to achieve some position in life. This genre had a long history in Egypt. The sage Imhotep wrote such a work, now lost, in the Third Dynasty and the latest surviving example, the *Instructions of Onkhsheshonqy*, is probably Ptolemaic. These wisdom texts are couched in the form of a discourse from a learned master, father or teacher to his pupil. A fair amount of the advice they contained inspired the scholar to diligence. In the words of the scribe Amenemope, 'pass no day in idleness or you will be beaten. The ear of a boy is on his back. He listens when he is beaten.'

Another type of text frequently found in school copies glorifies, rather smugly, the position of the scribe in society, by comparing with it, in a very poor light, all other crafts and trades. The most famous of these writings is the *Satire of the Trades*, in which are to be found such crushing comments as: 'I have seen the smith at work at the opening of his furnace; with fingers like claws of a crocodile, he stinks more than fish roe', and 'the potter is under the soil, though as yet among the living; he grubs in the mud more than a pig, in order to fire his pots'. By contrast, 'a scribe at whatever post in town, he will not suffer from it; as he fills another's need, he will not lack rewards … Behold! no scribe is short of food and of riches from the palace.'

A further source of information on the education, favoured status and potential power of the scribe is to be found in the *Miscellanies*, a group of short compositions collected on rolls of papyrus. These consist of texts, often in the form of open letters, concerning the workings

society was hierarchical and everyone owed duty to someone at a higher level, and ultimately to Pharaoh, who was the embodiment of the State. Nevertheless, at the bottom of the heap it becomes difficult to differentiate between the oppressed peasant labourer and those officially designated as slaves.

Unskilled peasant farmers were attached to an estate belonging to Pharaoh, the government, a temple or a rich landowner. Their pay was barely more than subsistence, or, if they cultivated land, a large percentage of the harvest was taken in rent and taxes. This group of people was the main target of *corvée* duty,

of administration and the life of the upper middle class of Egyptian society. They are full of unusual and technical language, mathematical problems and lists of exotica. As the *Kemyt* forms the basic primer, so the *Miscellanies* must represent the final stages of the scribe's education.

The final years of scribal training were probably vocational, either working with a master or attending one of the specialised schools run by the major employers of scribes such as the royal palace, government departments, the army or temples. In these schools the trainee would receive knowledge applicable to his future employment: mathematics and surveying for tax assessors, ritual practices or medicine for future priests, and so on.

At the other end of the social scale and at the lowest level of an Egyptian household were the servants and slaves who performed all the mundane duties, but who received little reward. To a certain extent the whole of Egypt was in a state of servitude, for the structure of

27 (*left*) School exercise written on an ostracon. Ostraca are flakes of stone or sherds of pottery which had been thrown away and were thus freely available for practising writing or drawing. Height 20.5 cm (no. 4154).

28 The stele of Sebeka shows a number of household slaves, designated by the word *djet*, employed in carrying food and baking bread. Height 60 cm (no. 1372).

29 Middle Kingdom tomb model showing domestic servants grinding corn on a saddle quern and baking bread in conical moulds over an open fire. Length 42 cm (no. 45197).

forced labour raised for specific tasks such as the upkeep of irrigation systems, construction of public buildings and cultivation of land. For this work no pay at all was received, only keep. All but the official classes were obliged to undertake the *corvée*, but anyone who could afford to do so would pay for exemption, thus ensuring that the weight of the burden fell on the poor. If, however, the *corvée* workers attempted to run away from their labour, they were classed as fugitives and, if caught, sentenced to permanent servitude, spending the time between jobs in prison. Their children then seem to have inherited the parents' status as State servants.

These unfortunates bridge the gap between the theoretically free peasants and the lowest class of Egyptian society, the slaves. Slavery is known to have existed in Egypt from the Middle Kingdom onwards. The majority of slaves were foreigners, either Asiatics or Nubians, usually captured in war, although some were brought into the country by merchants. There are a number of terms in Egyptian designating slaves, which basically differentiate between household and agricultural workers. Slaves could be bought, sold and hired like any other chattel, yet on the whole they appear to have been well treated and there are even examples of emancipated slaves marrying into their former owner's family. The majority of slaves were female, employed in domestic tasks. Yet not all domestic workers were slaves; many personal servants, as far as we can tell, were free to leave their employer or could be dismissed.

3 The Land and the River

In ancient Egypt the land and the river were inextricably linked, for without the annual inundation which irrigated and fertilised the soil, neither the prosperous economy nor the rich civilisation which it engendered could have existed. Furthermore, the Nile was the main highway of the country. Until the New Kingdom, transport on land was virtually non-existent. Donkeys were the only beasts of burden and travellers had to walk or be carried in a litter.

The inundation, which no longer affects Egypt since the construction of a series of dams and sluices from Aswan northwards, occurred during the summer, from July to October. It began with the fall of rain in central Sudan, which raised the level of the White Nile. A few weeks later, summer monsoon rains falling over the Ethiopian highlands caused a rapid swelling of the Blue Nile and the Atbara tributary. This excess of water reached Egypt in August, causing a dramatic rise in the level of the river. During late August and September the whole valley was flooded, apart from the higher areas of land on which the villages and towns were built. A fertile layer of silt was deposited over the fields and the parched soil was well soaked. The level of the inundation was crucial. If there was not enough water, insufficient ground would be prepared for the next season's crops and famine could ensue. Too much water caused severe damage to houses and dykes. The height of the flood could be predicted in advance using Nilometers constructed at various points along the river. By comparing the rate of rise with records kept over many centuries, the farmers would know whether to expect famine or plenty, or if they should move their belongings in a hurry.

As soon as the waters began to fall, the agricultural year began. First of all the fields had to be put back in order. This involved the repair of dykes and irrigation channels, the re-establishment of land boundaries and preparation of the soil. The re-establishment of field markers was important, not only to prevent legal wrangles over ownership of property, but for the assessment of taxes later in the year. To ensure that these essential tasks were carried out, the *corvée* system outlined in the previous chapter was instituted at a very early date. The unpleasant nature of the work led all those who could afford it to supply a deputy.

Once preparations were complete, the fields could be planted. The staple crops were emmer wheat, barley and flax. The cereal crops were for making bread and beer and the flax provided linen, from which the Egyptians made most of their clothes. Flax could be harvested at different times, depending on the use to which the fibres were to be put. The fibres from a young plant made fine thread, while those from a ripe plant were suitable for heavy fabric, rope-work and matting. The heads were removed by pulling them through a long comb-like tool and were used for seed, or possibly the manufacture of linseed oil. The stems

30 Wooden plough, shod with bronze. The lightness of its construction gives some idea of the ease with which the soil of Egypt could be turned. Length 93 cm (no. 50705).

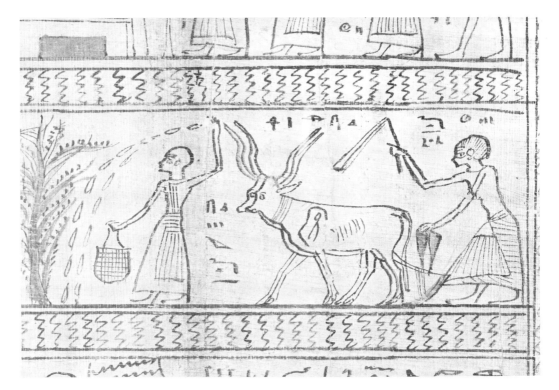

31 Ploughing and sowing took place at the same time, and sometimes the seed was broadcast before the path of the team, so that the plough planted the crop rather than simply preparing the ground for it (no. 9911, sheet 2).

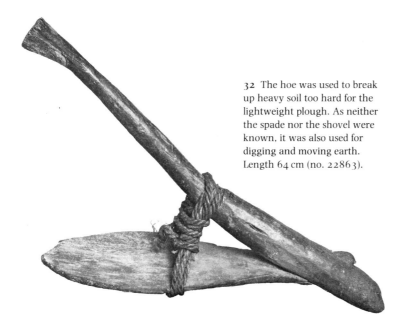

32 The hoe was used to break up heavy soil too hard for the lightweight plough. As neither the spade nor the shovel were known, it was also used for digging and moving earth. Length 64 cm (no. 22863).

were soaked to separate the wood from the fibres, then beaten to remove the wood, after which the fibres were combed out for spinning.

Ploughing and planting of all crops began in October. The plough was normally pulled by 30, 31 cows, not oxen, or even occasionally by men. It was guided from behind by the ploughman, who wielded a whip to encourage his team whilst pushing down on the plough with all his might with the other hand. The team was often guided at the front by an assistant, usually a boy or young man, using a stick or shouting encouragement. If the soil was exceptionally heavy or hard it was broken up 32 manually using hoes.

While the crops were ripening, work did not cease. Land away from the river might need further irrigation later in the season as the soil dried out. This was done using water from the

33 A senior tax assessor checking the limits of a field before beginning his survey. The tax would be assessed as a proportion of the expected yield from the area calculated. In front of him, horses and mules are harnessed to lightweight chariots. Height 4 3 cm (no. 37982).

34 Harvesting flax. As the whole stem was used, the harvesters pulled the entire plant bodily from the soil, taking care not to damage it (no. 10063, sheet 3).

network of canals that crossed the cultivated land. The water was led to the fields via small ditches separated from the canals by sluices. To get the water onto the soil, however, required heavy manual labour. No mechanical lifting system was known before the New Kingdom, when the *shaduf* was invented. This consisted of a tall upright post on which pivoted a long cross-pole, which could swing freely in all directions. At one end of the pole was a water container and at the other a heavy counterweight. The container was filled from the ditch and the weight raised the water to the required level. Unfortunately, this useful aid seems only to have been used to irrigate gardens, the labourer in the field having to continue this backbreaking task by hand. The *saqqieh*, or water wheel, commonly seen in Egypt today, did not appear until Ptolemaic times.

Other problems which the farmer had to contend with were pests, such as birds or insects, and flash storms which would flatten the grain as it ripened. The effects of these natural enemies are graphically described in the Biblical book of Exodus, in which the plagues visited on Egypt by the Hebrew god are catalogued. Against insects and the weather there was little recourse except prayer, but against the birds some action could be taken. Small boys were set in the fields, or in gardens, to make loud noises in order to scare the birds away. Spring traps were set to catch individual birds, but in the case of a whole flock descending, groups of men or boys would ensnare them in a large net and then kill them for food.

Towards harvest time other pests invaded the farmers' fields. These were the tax assess-
33 ors who came to gauge the yield of the crop and set the amount to be taken in dues.

The bustling activity of the harvest is shown
37 in a scene from the tomb of Menna at Thebes. The sequence begins on the left-hand side of

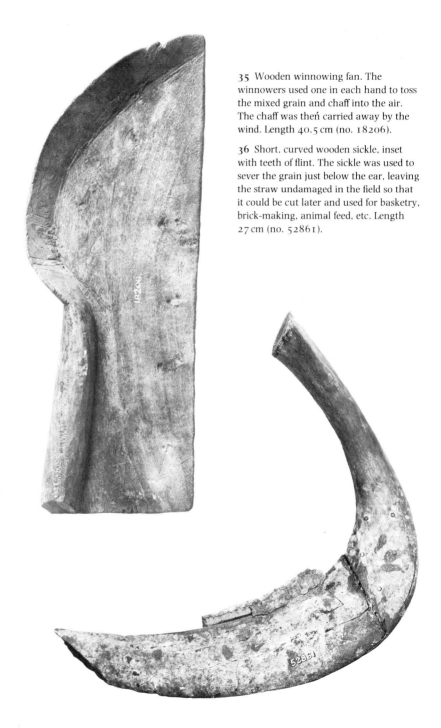

35 Wooden winnowing fan. The winnowers used one in each hand to toss the mixed grain and chaff into the air. The chaff was then carried away by the wind. Length 40.5 cm (no. 18206).

36 Short, curved wooden sickle, inset with teeth of flint. The sickle was used to sever the grain just below the ear, leaving the straw undamaged in the field so that it could be cut later and used for basketry, brick-making, animal feed, etc. Length 27 cm (no. 52861).

37 Harvest scene from the tomb of Menna at Thebes, showing the cutting of the grain and its removal to the threshing floor, where it is raked over before cattle trample the corn from the ears. The grain is then winnowed and counted by scribes. Copy by Nina de Garis Davies.

the bottom register. Menna sits beneath a shady baldachin watching the progress of his workmen, while a servant offers him a cool drink from a flask. In the field the harvesters are watched over by a scribe dressed in white linen. The men work with short, curved sickles. One of the labourers is seen taking a drink from a jar proffered by a young girl, while next to her another girl picks up gleanings dropped by the harvesters. Above the girls is a nursing mother, seated beneath a tree, with a bowl of food for the workers' break. Further along we see the harvested grain being taken from the field in large baskets carried on poles by pairs of men. At their feet children are gleaning and two girls fight over their finds. Gleaning by the families of field-workers was a traditional way of supplementing the low pay given by landowners. If they were able, the harvesters might intentionally drop ears for the benefit of the gleaners.

Beneath a tree slump a pair of idlers, one of whom is playing a flute. They may be harvesters taking a break or servants of Menna waiting for him to complete his inspection. At the end of the bottom register two men are shown forking over the ears of corn on the threshing floor prior to turning loose oxen to trample the grain from the chaff. This process is depicted at the beginning of the top register. A man drives a team of four beasts, while two others turn over the grain with forks. The next scene shows winnowing. A group of workers pick up the trampled ears in flat, wooden scoops, one in each hand. They toss the grain high in the air, causing the chaff to blow away in the wind, while the wheat falls back to the ground.

The final scene shows the scribes again at work, recording the harvest, measure by measure. It is now that the tax and rent, assessed earlier, are taken away. If the peasant

38 Agricultural techniques have changed very little in the more remote parts of Egypt. Compare this scene of winnowing with that in Menna's tomb painting.

could not or would not pay his dues, he was usually beaten mercilessly by order of these petty bureaucrats. Once the harvest was complete the grain was taken for storage in granaries.

The harvest was presided over by the goddess Renenutet, who is depicted as a cobra or a cobra-headed woman, as this snake was often found in ripe corn. In harvest scenes a swollen crescent shape is often shown above the winnowing floor. This may represent a type of corn-doll, perhaps another symbol of the harvest deity. The owner of the estate had to give her offerings of corn, birds, bread, cucumbers, melons and other fruit in thanks for a successful harvest, and no doubt other,

local deities also received a share of the bounty.

Many of the food crops cultivated by the ancient Egyptians needed constant watering and were therefore grown in irrigated gardens. Numerous varieties of plants were grown in this way, including fruits, green vegetables and beans. One of the main garden crops was the vine, used primarily for the production of wine, although grapes were also eaten, as well as raisins. The plants were often trained to form arbours or arches. Around the roots wells of mud were formed to help contain moisture. The grapes were harvested by hand, without the use of a knife, and carried gently to the press in rush baskets. They were emp-

39 Model granary, dating from the Middle Kingdom. Different types of cereal could be stored in separate silos, each of which had a sliding hatch near ground level. At the top of the stairs an overseer guards the valuable crop, while a servant grinds corn in the courtyard. Width 44 cm (no. 2463).

40 Lead beer siphon. As not all the solid residue could be filtered from the beer before it was decanted into jars, siphons were used as 'drinking straws'. The two pieces were connected by a reed, and another reed fitted into the other end of the angled tube, through which the drinker sucked. Height 10 cm and 7 cm (nos 55148–9).

41 Wine-making, from the tomb of Khaemwese at Thebes. The grapes are plucked gently and taken to the press. After primary fermentation, the wine is poured into jars, which are sealed with a fermentation lock. In the middle of the lower register, thank-offerings for the harvest are made to the goddess Renenutet, shown as a cobra. Copy by Nina de Garis Davies.

tied into vats large enough to contain up to six men, who would crush the grapes with their feet.

The grape juice flowed into a collecting vat, whence it was transferred into open pottery jars for primary fermentation. A second pressing, in a bag press, squeezed out the remaining juice from the skins, seeds and stems. After a vigorous primary fermentation in the open vessels, the wine was racked and transferred to other jars. These jars were sealed either with rush bung stoppers or with fermentation locks shaped like a saucer, with a hole in the centre to allow the gas to escape. The mouths and necks of the jars were almost entirely enveloped with mud capsules which were totally sealed after all the carbon dioxide had been released during the secondary fermentation. The jars were then labelled with information about date, type or use of the wine, estate, vineyard and vintner.

The main beverage of the ancient Egyptians, however, was beer. This was made from barley, which was first formed into a loaf and

42 Scene of cattle inspection. The herd contains the three types of cattle reared during the New Kingdom: long-horned and short-horned cattle and a hump-backed variety introduced from the Near East. Height 58.5 cm (no. 37976).

43 Marking the ownership of cattle by branding is known from the Eighteenth Dynasty. This bronze brand is probably that of an estate belonging to a temple of the goddess Sekhmet, perhaps near Thebes. Height 8.5 cm (no. 57321).

then half-baked so as to make the yeast active but not kill it. The loaves were then broken up and mixed with malted barley and water. The resultant mash was allowed to ferment for a few days and then sieved. The liquid was decanted into beer jars.

The Egyptians' staple food was bread, of which there were at least fifteen varieties in the Old Kingdom, whilst during the New Kingdom about forty names for breads, cakes and biscuits are attested. The difference between these various types was not only in the ingredients but also in shape, as the variety of surviving loaves indicates. The grinding of the grain for flour was a laborious process. It was first crushed in a large mortar, then sifted to remove the bran. The remainder was ground in a saddle quern, which consisted of a con- 29 cave quernstone over which a heavy stone rubber was passed back and forth. The flour was sieved and reground until it reached the required degree of fineness. Only sufficient for the daily bake was prepared. The most common type of loaf was conical, made in a mould which was placed over an open fire to cook. Dome-shaped ovens also existed, in which flat loaves could be baked by placing them against the hot interior of the dome.

The eating of meat was probably something of a luxury for most ancient Egyptians. Nevertheless, large numbers of animals were reared and domestication can be traced back to predynastic times. Cattle were the most common domestic animals, reared not only for their meat but also for dairy produce, as beasts of burden and for ritual use in sacrifice. Great herds were reared on temple domains as well as on royal and noble estates. The chief varieties were long-horned and short-horned cattle, but during the New Kingdom the hump-backed Brahminy bull was introduced from the Near East. Other domesticated animals reared for food were duck, geese, goats and pigs. During the Old Kingdom there were experiments in domesticating other animals, such as antelope, oryx and hyena, and these are sometimes depicted being force-fed in order to fatten them up. However, the experiments seem to have failed, for these creatures were never fully domesticated. Donkeys were also bred from an early time as beasts of burden but the camel was unknown until the Persian period. Horses did not appear in Egypt until the end of the Second Intermediate Period, introduced from the Near East. They were rarely ridden by the Egyptians, being used instead to pull chariots.

44 Middle Kingdom tomb model of a ship rigged for sailing upstream. Its owner is seen squatting before the mast, looking backwards. In the bows stands a pilot, while the crew work the sail. In the stern is a large steering oar pivoted on a wooden post. Length 113 cm (no. 25360).

Rarity restricted their ownership to Pharaoh, his nobles and the army.

For the main means of transport in ancient Egypt we turn once more to the river. A number of distinctive forms of boat were used to move both men and goods up and down the Nile, and as there were no bridges over the main stream, ferries operated back and forth incessantly. The wind in Egypt blows constantly from north to south and so when travelling to Upper Egypt vessels raised a large rectangular sail to power them against the current. The boats were steered by a large oar-like rudder or by pairs of oars along the sides, near the stern. When travelling downstream the sail was taken down, as the rectangular shape was of little use when tacking into the wind. The mast was dismantled and the boat propelled by rowers seated along the gunwhales, who were aided by the river's current.

Detailed models of passenger ships are found in Middle Kingdom tombs. They occur 44, 45 in pairs, one fully rigged, the other with the mast unstepped and the rowers in position. The tomb-owner was thus always prepared for travel both north and south in the afterlife. So established was this pattern of sailing that a ship under sail came to be the hieroglyph for travelling south (⛵) and a ship without sail or mast the hieroglyph for travelling north (⛵).

Another type of craft which must have been seen frequently on the river was the papyriform boat, whose shape was derived from the humble papyrus raft used for darting about along the banks and hunting in shallow, marshy waters. These papyriform boats had a strictly religious use, either for transporting a god from temple to temple or for carrying mummies and pious Egyptians on pilgrimage, usually to Abydos. The Egyptians also had sea-going vessels, known as 'Byblos ships' from the port in the Near East (in modern Lebanon) which they visited most frequently, trading for much-needed resources such as timber. These ships were very similar in form to the Nile passenger craft, but with extra strengthening members to withstand the strain of sailing in the open sea. A fleet of such vessels is depicted in a scene in the mortuary temple of Hatshepsut at Deir el-Bahri, representing a trading expedition which she sent to Punt, modern Somaliland, to obtain spices, incense trees and rare animals.

4 Crafts and Craftsmen

In contrast with today's craftsman, who is seen as an individual artist whose signed works have great intrinsic worth, his ancient Egyptian counterpart remained an anonymous artisan who was an object of derision to the arrogant scribal class. Most craftsmen in ancient Egypt were employed by Pharaoh, the government or temples. They laboured in large, highly organised workshops or in special communities, such as that of the royal tomb-builders at Deir el-Medina. Their techniques and tools were simple, the high quality of their achievement relying on their skill and the almost endless time and patience which they were able to devote to their work.

An example of such a workshop, belonging to a temple, comes from the tomb of two sculptors named Apuki and Nebamun at Thebes. They both held important positions as controllers of sculptors and artisans at the palace and in an unnamed temple, as well as being controllers of the balances of the king. All these posts had been held by their respective fathers before them.

In the top left of the scene, the supervisor is shown seated on a lattice-work stool. He is inspecting a number of finished pieces presented by two craftsmen. These include wooden furniture, a scribe's palette, metal vessels and jewellery. Above the two attendants is a man operating a balance. On one side are ten gold rings and on the other a weight in the form of a bull's head. Crowning the balance is a head of the goddess of truth, Ma'at, to ensure that the metal is weighed truly. This weighing of metal in the presence of an overseer represents one of the strict security measures which operated in these official workshops. All metal was precious to the ancient Egyptians. It was either rare or else the mining of it required great effort. Gold, for instance, was relatively abundant in Egypt and Nubia, but mining techniques were unsophisticated and the mines lay in inhospitable desert regions. Thus all raw metal given out to craftsmen was weighed and the amount recorded. Even simple bronze tools were registered out to the workmen at Deir el-Medina. The superintendent of a group of artisans, therefore, held a post of great responsibility and trust, which, as the records show, was unfortunately often abused.

The rest of the scene shows the activities of the workshop, or possibly series of workshops, conflated into one picture. It is a model of order and cleanliness, suitable for an idealised picture of the afterlife. In reality most workshops must have been noisy, dirty and hot, the ground littered with the debris of manufacture. The top register shows a group of carpenters and cabinet-makers at work. They are engaged in constructing a gilded shrine for the temple or a tomb. On the far right a balding man is seen cutting up wood into planks. The wood to be cut is held upright on a post by thick rope. The saw is pulled backwards and forwards, although unlike modern saws which cut on both actions, the ancient Egyptian saw cut only when pulled.

Behind the sawyer and on the far side of the men assembling the shrine are five artisans engaged in making amulets to decorate it. One of them roughly shapes a block of wood to the required size, while three others carve out the amulets. The main tool is the adze, which was used by the ancient Egyptians for cutting, shaping and smoothing wood. For finer work one man uses a chisel. The fifth craftsman is about to paint the *djed*-amulet (denoting strength) in his hand. Most of the men are seated on three-legged stools characteristic of artisans' workshops. They work on large blocks of stone or wood, some with ledges or stops to prevent their work slipping. In the centre two men place the completed amulets in the framework of the shrine. These appear smaller than the amulets in the process of manufacture, but this is because the latter have been enlarged by the artist so that they

47 A workshop, from the tomb of Apuki and Nebamun at Thebes. The crafts depicted include carpentry and cabinet-making, jewellery and metal-working. At the top left, finished articles are inspected, while gold rings are weighed before being issued to the craftsmen.

48 Set of carpenter's tools from a Theban tomb, consisting of an axe for trimming and splitting wood, a pull-saw, adzes, chisels, bradawls and a bow-drill, as well as a honing stone and an oil flask. With such tools, very fine joinery was possible.

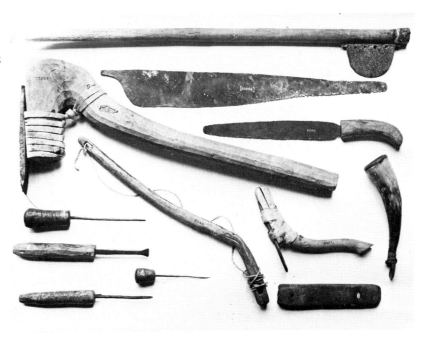

49 A bronze vessel shaped by hammering over a rod-anvil, probably using a rounded stone covered with cloth or leather to soften the blows. The hammer marks form a textured decoration on the surface. Height 24 cm (no. 57288).

50 The shape of this bronze bowl would have been obtained by hammering, and the decoration of *ankh*-signs and uraei chased into the metal rather than engraved. The technique of engraving was not used until iron became common in the Late Period. Diameter 15 cm (no. 51462).

can be more clearly seen.

The techniques of carpentry were similar to those of today. Wood was joined by dovetailing, mitreing, mortice and tenon joints and dowels. Inlay and veneer were common forms of decoration, as a means of disguising the poor native timbers of Egypt. Ebony and ivory were glued or pinned to the surface of the object. Paint was also used, applied over a thin layer of gesso. There is even one example of plywood used to construct a Third Dynasty coffin, a technique not used again until modern times.

In the central and lower registers are depicted metalworkers and jewellers. Two men, seated on stools, prepare and place in a box elaborate pectorals and necklaces. The one on the right rubs together two pieces of inlay in order to smooth them. An abrasive substance is kept in the cup above his hands. Above this is a bowl containing semi-precious stones

awaiting use, covered with a cloth to keep away prying eyes. His companion places a pectoral containing the cartouches of Amenophis III in a casket. Other jewels ready for packing are shown above.

Next to this pair are two men engaged in chasing and carving metal, one of whom is named as the draughtsman of the god Amun, Pasinisu, also called Parennefer. He chases an inscription on a libation vessel, while his friend works on a golden sphinx using a stone hammer and metal chisel. Further along metal vessels are being manufactured: the smaller of the two is supported on a rod-anvil, while the smith beats it with a stone hammer. Above the smith's head are completed vessels, possibly awaiting further embellishment by the chasers. On the far right a smith heats a partially worked vessel in a small furnace. This process was required to keep the metal supple, as copper and bronze become brittle when

49, 50

beaten. He holds the metal with a pair of tongs, whilst blowing through a tube to raise the temperature in the furnace.

The lower register is damaged, but enough remains to show that, on the left, bronze lamp stands are in the process of manufacture. One of the smiths heats a small piece of metal in a fire on the ground, again raising the temperature by means of a blow-pipe. Behind him two men appear to be beating a metal sheet over a concave form, possibly the preliminary shaping of a vessel. In the centre of the register is an elaborate furnace in which metal is smelted from the ingots shown above, probably copper and tin combined to make bronze. The furnace is aerated by four men operating foot bellows. These were presumably made of leather. The men hold ropes in their hands, on which they pull to reflate the bellows after they have trodden out the air.

The molten metal from the furnace would probably have been used for casting, although this process is not shown in the scene. Copper and bronze were used for casting tools, weapons and decorative objects, using moulds cut out of stone or fashioned from pottery. Cast metal was also used for figure statuettes, although not commonly until the Late Period. The British Museum's bronze statuette of Tuthmosis IV is a rare example from the Eighteenth Dynasty. The technique used for casting these figures was the lost-wax process. This method could be used to make either solid cast or hollow figurines, the latter representing a way of economising on the valuable metal.

On the far right of the lower register is a group of stone-workers engaged in the manufacture of beads and vessels. In order to make beads, suitable pieces of coloured or semi-precious stone were broken up and roughly shaped by rolling or bruising. They were then smoothed by rubbing them together. The next phase was to bore holes through the beads for

51

51 Bronze statuette of Tuthmosis IV made by the lost-wax process. The form of the object was moulded in wax and covered with clay. The clay was heated to harden it, and the wax melted, running out through holes in the clay. Molten metal could then be poured into the rigid mould. Height 14.5 cm (no. 64564).

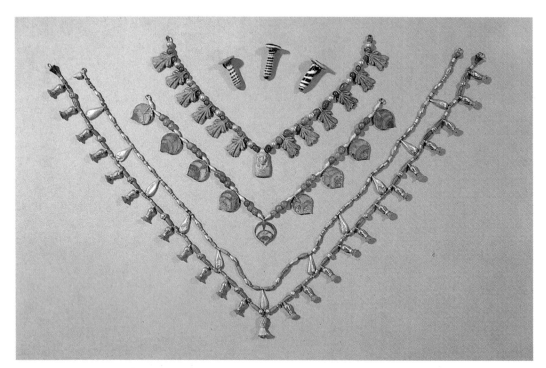

52 A selection of necklaces and earplugs. The Egyptians favoured brightly coloured costume jewellery, using a wide range of materials but not precious stones. Instead, they used semi-precious stones, glazed composition and even glass.

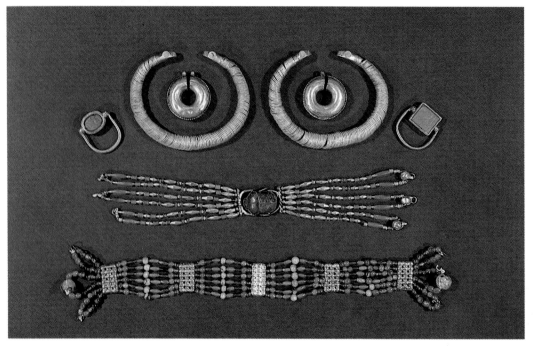

53 Bracelets, bangles, signet rings and earrings. Gold was plentiful in ancient Egypt and was used as the basis of much jewellery. These pieces show the delicate skill of the ancient craftsmen.

stringing. This was achieved using a bow-drill. The drill point of metal, stone or tough reed was attached to a stick. This was rotated using the string of the bow as the operator moved it backwards and forwards. Many beads were drilled from both sides. If one hole began to wander off true, another was begun from the other side to meet it. For this reason ancient beads rarely have straight holes running through them. The drill bit was aided by an abrasive material such as emery or fine quartz, which is shown on the table next to the drill worker. To speed up production several bits were operated by the same drill – one reason, no doubt, why the line of the bore ran out of true so frequently. Once the beads were made they could be polished or glazed as required. They were then handed over to craftsmen who made them into simple strings of beads, elaborate collars or amuletic nets and plaques to be placed on mummies.

The Egyptians mastered the techniques of making fine stone vessels at an early date, utilising the great range of ornamental stone 54 to be found in the desert and hills which border the Nile. A block of stone would be cut to the appropriate dimensions, probably with a saw. The shape of the vessel was then roughly formed with a chisel or a drill. Smoothing followed, using abrasive stone rubbers worked up and down the object. When the outside was completely shaped, the inside was hollowed out. This was achieved using a drill with an offset crank handle at the top, as shown in the scene. The drill was set with a stone bit of flint, limestone, sandstone or diorite shaped for different types of vessel or phases of the work. Some drill bits were formed of copper tubes which could remove cylindrical cores. A chisel could then be used to remove the surrounding material. Some vessels were made in sections and then cemented together. This applied especially to ornate vessels with narrow mouths. As with bead drilling, emery or quartz was used as an abrasive.

The techniques of sculpting were not very different. The outline of a statue was marked on an appropriate piece of stone with red ochre. The piece was then roughly blocked out 55 and the features modelled. In the case of soft stones such as limestone, chisels could be used as well as saws. Hard, volcanic stones could only be worked with similarly dense materials. The amount of time, patience and manpower used to create a colossal statue of granite almost defies the modern imagination.

Among other craft techniques not depicted in the tomb of Apuki and Nebamun, the manufacture of glass and glazed ware is 57 characteristically Egyptian. Glazed composition (faience) is known from the predynastic period onwards. It consists of quartz ground to a fine powder, possibly mixed with a weak solution of natron to make the material malleable. Objects of glazed composition could be formed by hand or on a wheel, but many small

54 Stone vessels. Egyptian craftsmen used a wide variety of stone, but chiefly alabaster (calcite), granite, breccia, basalt, schist, serpentine and steatite. Despite their lack of hard cutting tools, they were able to manipulate their unyielding medium with great dexterity, creating elaborate forms effectively hollowed out inside.

pieces were shaped in pottery moulds. The glaze was similar in composition to glass, being made of sand and natron salt. It was probably applied as a fluid coating which fused with the body material on firing, creating an object of great strength. The usual colour for the glaze was blue-green or turquoise, created by the inclusion of copper or malachite. Nevertheless, it was possible to produce other colours: objects of red, white, yellow and green proliferate during the late Eighteenth Dynasty.

Although the glaze used on faience is similar in composition to glass, glass proper was not made in Egypt until the Eighteenth Dynasty and it seems likely that the technique was introduced from Syria. Glass production involved the heating together of quartz and natron with a colouring compound, usually a copper-based blue. The molten glass could be moulded, shaped into rods or formed round a core, but blown glass was not known until the Roman period. Core-forming involved the creation of a sandy core in the shape of the inside of the intended vessel. This was then dipped into the molten glass and twirled round, creating a skin of uneven thickness which could be worked to the required shape. Bases and handles were added separately. Decoration in different colours was often applied in the form of rods of glass which melted on contact with the hot body of the vessel. A tool drawn across the bars of colour created a ripple-pattern effect.

Weaving was another major craft of the ancient Egyptians, dating back to early pre-dynastic times. The cloth they used was made of linen, and the cultivation and treatment of flax has already been described. The linen fibre, having been beaten from the plant, was spun on a stick weighted at one end with a circular whorl, either flat or domed. Until the New Kingdom, women alone spun thread, but thereafter men also took part in this operation. The same is true of weaving. The loom in

56

Egypt was at first horizontal, but was replaced by a vertical type during the Second Intermediate Period. A great variety of cloth was produced, from coarse homespun to a fine linen, as sheer as muslin, known as *byssos*. Most cloth was plain, although sometimes a pattern of loose threads was woven in.

Allied to weaving was the manufacture of mats, baskets and rope using reed, flax, papyrus, palm fibre and grass. Mats were woven on horizontal looms, while baskets were made by coiling a fibrous core spirally into the shape required. Baskets were as common as pottery in the Egyptian home and were used as con-

55 (*left*) Unfinished basalt statuette of a queen or goddess, showing how the form of the piece was first roughly shaped by pecking and gouging. Late Period, *c.* 600 BC. Height 32 cm (no. 55251).

56 Core-formed and blown glass objects. Glass was used for luxury items such as cosmetic vessels, as well as jewellery and inlays. The technique of glass-blowing did not appear in Egypt until the Roman period.

57 Glazed composition (faience) could be moulded and therefore used for mass production. It was most commonly used for vessels such as bowls and chalices, jewellery, tiles, inlays and *shabti* figures, placed in tombs as magical servants of the dead.

tainers for food, clothing and household linen. Nevertheless, a great deal of pottery was made and used by the ancient Egyptians, although it was not a craft at which they excelled. The best pottery belongs to the late predynastic age, when fine black and red wares were produced, as well as vessels boldly painted in red on buff. It was not until the Eighteenth Dynasty that painted wares reappeared, the most striking examples being blue-painted buff vessels especially common during the reigns of Amenophis III and Akhenaten.

Let us return once again to the craftsmen who created some of these works of art in ancient Egypt and take a look at the organisation of one particular group about which we have a lot of information: the tomb-builders of Deir el-Medina. These artisans were divided into two groups, the left and the right gangs, which presumably worked on the left- and right-hand sides of the tomb at the same time. The gangs were controlled by two foremen who were appointed by the vizier, although the posts became hereditary. The son of the foreman often became his father's deputy before taking over full responsibility for the gang. Working with the foreman was an official scribe who administered the activities of the workmen and the village. He oversaw the distribution of tools and materials from the royal stores, carefully registering what was given to each man. He also kept lists of those who were not at work and the reason for their absence and, most importantly, he received and distributed the men's wages. Below the scribe was a guardian who looked after the official stores, while other guardians acted as watchmen over the tomb under construction. These would be supplemented as necessary by the official police of western Thebes, the Medjay.

The main body of the workforce consisted of stonemasons, plasterers, sculptors, draughtsmen, painters and carpenters. They worked for eight days out of ten, living in huts above

58 (*top*) Baskets were commonly used as containers in ancient Egyptian households. They were usually made of palm leaves coiled spirally into the shape required, or of papyrus and cane, and could be decorative as well as functional.

59 Predynastic pottery vessels were hand-made by coiling, but could nevertheless be of very high quality. Note the moulded lizard on the right-hand pot. Painted decoration died out on native pottery at the end of the predynastic period.

the Valley of the Kings and returning to the village for their two days of rest. During the day they were supposed to work for eight hours with a mid-day meal break but absenteeism was frequent. Days were lost for such reasons as brewing beer, building houses and drinking, and these, added to the large number of religious holidays, show that the tomb-builders in fact only worked for about six months of the year. Their payment was in kind: wheat and barley for making bread and beer, water, fish, vegetables, cosmetic oils, wood for fuel, pottery and clothing. On festival days they were given more elaborate food, including wine, as well as bonuses of oil, salt and meat. In order to help prepare these foodstuffs a number of female slaves were assigned to the village. At times the delivery of these essentials became irregular, or ceased altogether. On several occasions the men actually went on strike to demand that their wages be sent. Nevertheless, these 'servants of the place of truth', as they were at one time called, were comparatively well off. They used their skills to construct highly decorated tombs for each other. There were also opportunities for moonlighting – making tombs or funerary equipment for the well-to-do of Thebes. Their houses were well appointed and their lists of possessions, as we have already seen, could be relatively impressive. Of the living standards of other craftsmen we unfortunately know little, but it is to be suspected that by and large they were less comfortable.

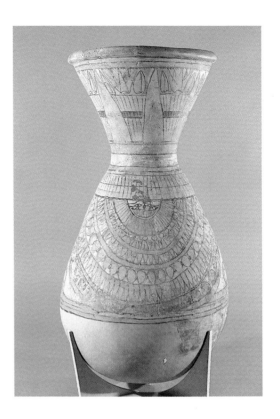

60 Large painted jar from El-Amarna. Native pottery in the dynastic period was purely utilitarian until the Eighteenth Dynasty, when painted wares reappeared. This jar is painted in light blue on a buff background, with details picked out in red and black. Designs are usually based on floral patterns. Height 70 cm (no. 56841).

61 Artist's trial piece from the Theban necropolis, showing the head of a lion and four chicks, elaborate forms of common hieroglyphs. Practice pieces such as this may have been done by apprentices or by craftsmen making a rough draft before committing a design to a tomb wall. Length 16 cm (no. 26706).

5 Dress

The dress of the ancient Egyptians consisted not simply of the clothes they wore but also of elaborate costume jewellery which served to embellish their usually plain garments, wigs which they wore over their own cropped hair, and striking cosmetics which not only enhanced their features but were also thought to have hygienic and medicinal qualities. Their clothing was simple and did not change a great deal over the millennia, although more elaborate styles did appear during the New Kingdom. The universal material was linen, which was light and cool to wear. Wool seems almost never to have been used, possibly because of religious taboos, although the native Egyptian sheep were not wool-bearing, and cotton was unknown until the Coptic period. Garments were draped round the body rather than tailored, and sewing was kept to a minimum. The chief form of decoration was pleating, and from examples of garments which have survived it is clear that a mechanical process was used to put the small, regular pleats into the cloth and that some form of starch or size was used to fix them. The nature of the implement which created the pleats is unknown, but it may have consisted of a board cut in peaks and grooves into which the cloth was pressed.

Coloured or patterned cloth was rarely used.

62 Dancing girls wearing patterned garments, from the tomb of Qenamun at Thebes. Most of the coloured garments depicted, especially before the New Kingdom, are worn by foreigners or servants. Copy by Nina de Garis Davies.

63 (*left*) Man wearing the basic linen kilt, made of a piece of cloth wrapped round the body and knotted at the waist. Height 62 cm (no. 35261).

64 (*right*) Calf-length kilt fashionable during the Middle Kingdom. It has horizontal pleats or fold-marks, as well as vertical lines which may also be fold-marks. Height 23 cm (no. 58180).

One reason for this is that it is very difficult to fix dyes into linen without a mordant, the use of which was unknown in ancient Egypt. Garments with coloured patterns are depicted in 62 tombs and a few examples have survived, but the technique of their production was not native. It was developed in the Near East and only brought into Egypt with the introduction of the vertical loom. The use of woven patterned textiles by the Egyptians was never widespread and may have been limited to the royal household.

Let us briefly survey the changing fashions of ancient Egypt up to the New Kingdom, after which there was little change or development. The basic costume for men, throughout the period, was a kilt, falling to just above the knee 63 and made of a rectangular piece of linen folded round the body and tied at the waist with a knot or fastened with a buckle. Variations on this simple theme include a squared end, a rounded end, a starched front forming an apron, and pleating. In the Old Kingdom this is the only type of male costume depicted, although a cloak of some sort must have been added for cool weather. Official and ceremonial attire was more complicated. Priests, for example, wore leopard skins wrapped around their torso and falling over the kilt like an apron. Working men often wore only a twist of linen around their loins or went naked. Children are also frequently depicted naked, as are those indulging in rigorous exercise.

Women wore simple sheath dresses falling from the breast to just above the ankle. These 67 appear to have been made of a rectangle of material sewn down one side, roughly hemmed and with straps attached to the top edge to support the dress. Their extreme figure-hugging style may be put down partly to artistic licence – the desire of the artist to show the form of the body beneath. Examples of dresses which survive from the Early Period are much more baggy and have sleeves. Indeed, if the dresses were as tight as portrayed, they would have been difficult to put on, let alone walk in.

During the Middle Kingdom pleated clothing became far more common and although men continued to wear the short kilt, a longer, straighter style appeared which was fastened on the chest and fell to the shins. Representations of this type of kilt indicate a series of wide, horizontal pleats, which may in reality have been fold-marks in the cloth. These 'maxi-kilts' were frequently worn over the top of a short under-kilt. At this time clothing for the upper part of the body is also shown. It consists of a bag-like tunic made simply from a rectangle of material seamed up the sides, with holes left for the arms and another hole cut in the centre for the head. An enveloping cloak also appears, wrapped round the body, although one shoulder was sometimes left bare. The edges of this garment are frequently fringed. The style of female dress changed little during the Middle Kingdom, although colours and patterning became popular among working women.

The New Kingdom heralded the appearance of a highly elaborate style of dress for both men and women. Pleating ran riot and is to be seen over the whole garment. Fringing also became more popular. Men usually wore a short under-kilt, over which hung a long, heavily pleated skirt, knotted at the hips, with a fringed sash hanging down over a pleated apron which fell below the knee. On their torso they wore a developed form of the bag-tunic, with a key-hole neck and wide sleeves which were normally pleated, although plain tight sleeves are also shown. A light shawl or cloak was sometimes thrown over the shoulder.

The greatest leap forward was in women's dress, which became far more elegant, although it took its form from men's fashions rather than developing a style of its own. The

65 Linen tunic made from a single piece of cloth folded and stitched down the sides, with holes left for the arms and another cut for the neck. It was probably worn as an undergarment. Length 120 cm (no. 2565).

66 Man wearing a cloak of a kind which became popular in the Middle Kingdom. The edges are fringed and one shoulder left bare. Underneath the cloak, a long kilt would probably have been worn. Height 16 cm (no. 36441).

67 (right) Woman wearing a tight sheath dress with two broad straps, which leave her breast bare. This style is typical of the Old and Middle Kingdoms. Colour is added to her plain costume by the blue diadem, collar, bracelets and anklets. Twelfth Dynasty. Height 71 cm (no. 1150).

sheath dress was still worn, but often only as an undergarment. On top is to be found a heavily pleated, fringed robe. This seems to have been made of a single piece of cloth draped over the body, without any stitching. The material was folded round the waist and the two top corners pulled over the shoulders. A knot was tied under the breasts to hold the garment in place.

On their feet the ancient Egyptians wore sandals made of woven reed, grass or leather. The standard form consisted of a thong passing between the first and second toes and attached to a bar passing over the instep. In the Nineteenth Dynasty a style with an upturned toe appeared, a forerunner of the Turkish slipper. Among the earliest examples of this type 18 are the delicate, red leather sandals found in the cosmetic chest of the lady Tutu, wife of the scribe Ani.

An integral part of Egyptian costume was a wig or hairpiece added to the natural hair. Many Egyptians shaved their heads or cropped their hair very short, although some did retain a full head of hair which they kept elaborately dressed. Sculpture and wall scenes show that there was a great variety of hairstyles to choose from, both for everyday wear and festive occasions. There does, however, seem to have been an element of idealisation in the rendering of wigs, as there was in clothing, for surviving examples are far less elegant than their regular, sculpted counterparts.

Wigs were made of human hair, although some vegetable-fibre padding was also used. The wig illustrated has a mass of lightish curls 68 on top and a multitude of thin, tight plaits below ear level. The foundation for these elements was a net woven of plaited human hair, with rhomboidal openings. The wig comprises about 300 strands, each of which contains about 400 individual hairs. These have been coated with a mixture of beeswax and resin. To attach the strand to the net, some of the

68 Elaborate wig with a mass of light-coloured curls on top of plaits. The wig is made of human hair and would have been worn on festive or official occasions. Length 50.5 cm (no. 2560).

hairs were looped over the netting while the rest of the strand was whipped round the loop. This was then waxed to fix the strand in place. The melting point of the wax is about 60 degrees Celsius, so it was unlikely to melt even on the hottest Egyptian day.

The manufacture and care of these wigs, as well as the creation of elaborate plaited hairstyles, required either the specialist services of a hairdresser for those who could afford it, or the help of a friend for those who could not. A number of scenes and figurines survive showing ladies at their coiffure. Pins rather than combs seem to have been used to arrange and hold the tight curls, although combs, both functional and decorative, have been found in large numbers.

The Egyptians were fastidious about the rest of their bodily hair, considering a hirsute ap-pearance a sign of uncleanliness and personal neglect. The only exceptions to this were an occasional thin moustache or goatee type of beard on men. For this reason, the razor had a long history in Egypt, beginning in predynastic times. Originally there were two types: an asymmetrical variety with a single cutting edge at the side, and a symmetrical, spatula-like type with parallel sides and a rounded cutting edge. The asymmetrical type soon fell out of use, but the spatula type survived and developed through a series of forms. The sides began to splay out, and during the Middle Kingdom the cutting edge began to protrude laterally. By the New Kingdom this had evolved into a hatchet-like form with a handle at a virtual right angle to the cutting edge and a spur projecting from the rear. This is thought to have served as a counter-weight to ensure proper balance in the handling. The exact mode of handling and method of working the razors has not yet been fully established. In the absence of soap, oil or unguent was probably used to soften the skin and hairs of the area to be shaved.

Other types of implement were available for removing unwanted hair. Tweezers are known from the First Dynasty onwards, with both sharp and blunt ends for different tasks. There are also curious composite tools consist-ing of two metal elements pegged together with a pin. One element is straight-edged with a sharp point at one end, and the other has a flat blade and a razor-like blade. These imple-ments may well have served several purposes. It has been suggested that they acted as curl-ing tongs, but they were certainly used as razors for close, delicate work.

Vain of their appearance, the ancient Egyp-tians considered cosmetics an important part of their dress. Nevertheless, their use went beyond this, for their application was often a matter of personal hygiene and health. Oils and creams were of vital importance against the hot Egyptian sun and dry, sandy winds. So essential were they considered that non-arrival of ointments in part-payment of wages was one of the chief grievances of the striking workers at Deir el-Medina during the reign of Ramesses III. The oils were necessary to keep the skin soft and supple and to prevent the onset of ailments caused by cracked, dry skin. Thus ointments figure largely in medical recipes of all kinds throughout Egyptian history.

A great variety of oils and fats were available to the ancient Egyptian perfumers. These can be identified in texts and from the writings of Classical authors such as Theophrastus, Dioscorides and Pliny. The most popular basic oil was *balanos* and the most widespread the castor oil used by the poor. The Egyptians were fond of strong scents, which they would blend with the base oils and animal fats to form perfumes. It is certain that the modern process of distillation using steam was not known for the extraction of essences,

but there were three techniques available for producing perfumes from flowers, fruits and seeds.

The first of these was *enfleurage*, the saturation of layers of fat with perfume by steeping flowers in the fat and replacing them when their perfume was spent. In this way the Egyptians were able to create creams and pomades. A popular form of pomade was the so-called cosmetic cone which was worn on top of the head. They are frequently represented in banqueting scenes, worn not only by the guests but also by the servants. The cone is usually white with streaks of orange-brown running from its top. The colouring represents the perfume with which the cone was impregnated. As the evening progressed, the cone would melt and the scented oil run down over the wig and garment, creating a pleasing scent and, no doubt, a sticky mess. Throughout the course of an evening, it became necessary to renew the scent on the cones and the tomb scenes show servants circulating among the guests, replenishing the perfumed cream.

The second process for creating perfume was maceration, that is dipping flowers, herbs or fruits into fats or oils heated to a temperature of about 65 degrees Celsius. This technique is depicted in a number of tomb scenes. The flowers or fruits were pounded in mortars and then stirred into the oil, which was kept hot on a fire. The mixture was sieved and allowed to cool. It might then be shaped into balls or cones, or, if liquid, poured into vessels. An alternative process may have been to macerate the flowers in water, cover the vessel with a cloth impregnated with fat and boil the contents of the vessel until all the perfumes had evaporated, fixing them in the fat which was then scraped off the cloth. This technique is still used by peoples living near the source of the Nile.

Thirdly, there was the possibility of expressing the flowers or seeds. This process was bor-

69 A decorative comb, a large pin for dressing wigs, a razor, tweezers and a multiple tool for removing unwanted facial and body hair.

rowed from the manufacture of wine and oil. The material to be pressed was placed in a bag with a stick attached to each end. The sticks were twisted in opposite directions, exerting pressure on the contents. In a more sophisticated form, the bag was attached to a frame at one end. The other end was held by a stick which was twisted by a group of workmen. This technique was not used often, as most recipes specify either maceration or *enfleurage.*

Eye paint is probably the most characteristic of the Egyptian cosmetics. Two colours were popularly used: black and green. The use of these pigments for the eyes dates back as far as the Badarian period (*c.* 4000 BC). Both colours have been found in early graves as fragments of raw material, often in small bags, as stains on palettes or in the prepared state as a dried paste or powder. The prepared eye paint has been found in shells, in segments of hollow reed, wrapped in plant leaves or in small vases. The green pigment is malachite, an oxide of copper. In the Early Period this was the most popular colour, and especially in the Old Kingdom when it was applied liberally from the eyebrow to the base of the nose. In the Middle

Kingdom green eye paint continued to be used for the brows and corners of the eyes, but by the New Kingdom it had been superseded almost entirely by black. Black eye paint (kohl), which was usually made of galena, a sulphide of lead, was used in the Early Period, but did not come into its own until the late Middle and New Kingdoms. It then continued right through to the Coptic period. By this time, however, soot was the basis of the black pigment.

Both the malachite and galena were ground on a palette and then mixed with either water or gum and water to form a paste. It is assumed that before the Middle Kingdom the kohl was applied with the fingers, but at this time kohl pencils begin to appear. These take the form of slender sticks with a bulbous end. They are made from wood, bronze, haematite, obsidian or glass. Some examples have a spatula end for mixing, or even a tiny spoon. The sticks are frequently attached to containers and act as a means of fastening the lid.

In the predynastic period and Old Kingdom, eye paint was kept in a variety of different vessels and was probably often mixed just

70 A group of cosmetic objects. At the back are decorative eye-paint pots and tubes and at the front two eye-paint applicators. The duck-shaped box and exquisite floral spoon probably contained cosmetic creams.

1658

71 A multiple eye-paint pot which may have contained medicinal eye paint, for its tubes are inscribed with instructions for use during the different seasons of the year, when different eye diseases were prevalent. Height 8 cm (no. 5337).

72 Fragmentary stele of the lady Ipwet, who is shown looking in a mirror and applying a cosmetic to her face with a cloth. This may be a face powder or red ochre to add colour to her cheeks. Length 50 cm (no. 1658).

prior to use. During the Middle and early New Kingdoms, however, kohl was almost invariably kept in a small jar or pot of special design with a flat bottom, wide rim, tiny mouth and flat, disc-shaped lid. The majority of kohl pots were made out of stone, especially alabaster, but other materials were also used, such as glazed composition, glazed steatite, glass, pottery and wood.

During the New Kingdom, the kohl pot was gradually replaced by a new type of container, which was a tube formed of a length of reed or a number of lengths bound together. This tubular form was imitated in other materials: wood, ivory, glazed composition, glass and stone. Multiple containers reproducing clusters of reeds became typical, usually in wood or stone.

From these basic forms there developed a series of decorative types. A common variety

has the form of a miniature palm column reproduced in polychrome glass with multi-coloured decoration. These columns also occur in glazed composition and ivory, with the variant design of a papyrus bud column. Squatting or standing monkeys holding kohl tubes appear quite frequently, as do human figures, either grotesques or young girls. Finally, images of the popular deity Bes figure on a number of containers in stone, glazed composition, ivory and wood.

Kohl was certainly used for its cosmetic value, making the eyes appear larger and more luminous, but the green eye paint also had a symbolic meaning, representing the eye of the god Horus, which was a potent amulet. Kohl may also have had a prophylactic function, the dark line around the eye stopping the glare of the sun. It was used as the basis for many eye medicines and is included in pre-

70

71

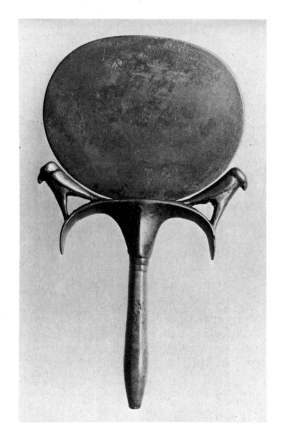

73 Bronze mirror with a handle in the form of a papyrus plant, on top of which stand two falcons. The metallic disc would have been highly polished, and its shining surface was likened by the ancient Egyptians to the disc of the sun. Length 24 cm (no. 32583).

coming from the Middle Kingdom. Mummies of dancers and royal concubines have geometric designs tattooed on their chests, shoulders, arms, abdomens and thighs. In the New Kingdom, dancers, musicians and servant girls occasionally had a tiny representation of the god Bes tattooed on their thighs as a good-luck charm.

The toilet object essential to all beautification is the mirror. In ancient Egypt mirrors 72, 73 took the form of highly polished metal discs, usually of bronze. Besides being functional, mirrors developed religious and funerary uses. Their circular shape, brightness and reflective quality suggested to the Egyptians the face of the sun and its life-giving powers and thus the mirror became a symbol of regeneration and vitality. The religious aspect is highlighted in the motifs used to decorate the handles. The papyrus plant, which figures frequently, is another symbol of vitality, as is the head of Hathor, a goddess of fertility and beauty. Metallic mirrors may have been restricted to the more well-to-do. For the poor a reflection in water had to suffice.

The final element of dress was jewellery, a 74 wide variety of which was worn by the ancient 52, 53 Egyptians. Although worn as personal adornment, much of the jewellery had an underlying amuletic purpose, to protect the wearer from harm – both tangible, in the form of dangerous creatures, and intangible evil forces which might invade the vulnerable points of the body. Thus many items of jewellery take the form of amulets. Even certain of the materials used had amuletic properties, notably carnelian, turquoise and lapis lazuli.

The most prominent types of costume jewellery were the collar and the pectoral worn at the neck. Collars were usually broad, covering much of the chest. They were made up of rows of beads, either plain, amuletic or floral. The strings of the various rows passed through large terminals which were themselves orna-

scriptions against eye diseases to be found in the medical papyri.

To colour their cheeks the Egyptians used red ochre in a base of fat or gum-resin. Ochre may have been used as lipstick, and a scene in a papyrus now in Turin shows a woman painting her lips with a brush whilst holding a container in her hand. Henna was used as a colourant, as it is today. It was certainly used to colour hair and perhaps also the palms of the hands, soles of the feet and nails, although it has been suggested that the henna-like stain on these parts of mummies was caused by embalmers' materials.

Tattooing was known and practised by the ancient Egyptians, the earliest direct evidence

mental or amuletic, common forms being lotus flowers or falcon heads. The weight of these heavy collars was supported at the back by a counterpoise pendant called a *mankhet*. The pectoral developed from a single amuletic pendant hanging from a cord round the neck into a large plaque with án amuletic motif, usually a deity or a large scarab. It was worn with bead necklaces or straps. A great variety of less broad and elaborate necklaces were also worn.

Head ornament took the form of diadems or filets based on bands of live flowers, but the floral forms were also copied in metal and semi-precious stones. Earrings did not appear in Egypt until the beginning of the New Kingdom and they soon became quite elaborate. They were worn through wide holes punched in the ear lobes. Plain, mushroom-shaped ear plugs, usually made of stone, glass or glazed composition, were also popular.

Limb ornaments consisted of armlets, bracelets and anklets, although a combination of all three was not worn until the New Kingdom and men did not wear anklets until the Ramesside age. Early types were made of shell, ivory or beads, but they developed into opulent, inlaid metal jewels designed to be worn in pairs. The Egyptians also wore finger rings. The most usual variety was a signet ring formed of a button seal or scarab, but other amuletic types were also popular. Most of the rings which survive are made of glazed composition, the design being cast in a mould. Nevertheless, heavy metal signet rings with figures of deities, royal names and protective hieroglyphs are also common.

74 This unusual mummy mask gives a good idea of the way in which an Egyptian lady wore her jewellery. Round her wig are diadems of floral design, and she wears large earrings. Around her neck is a wide bead collar; on her arms are two pairs of heavy bracelets, and her fingers are encrusted with rings. Length 58 cm (no. 6665).

6 Recreation

The ancient Egyptians were a people who knew how to enjoy themselves, as the great number and variety of pastimes recorded in tomb scenes so vividly illustrates. Indeed, it was to a large extent the intense pleasure which they found in life that encouraged them to seek to continue it after death.

Let us begin with the more active, sporting pursuits. Hunting for pleasure in the desert or marshland was the sport of Pharaoh, his nobles and the well-to-do. In early days a desert hunt took place on foot, but following the introduction of the chariot the nobleman galloped away in pursuit of his prey armed as if for war. The technique of hunting was to await or lure a large number of animals to a restricted area, possibly around a water hole, and then to attack them en masse with volleys of arrows. The nobleman would be accompanied by professional huntsmen. Hunting dogs were let loose to harry the hapless prey. The early hunting dogs had erect, pointed ears, narrow flanks and a short, curled tail, while in the New Kingdom there appeared a breed with pendent ears and long, straight tail, like the modern saluki. A very early hunting scene is shown in the Hunters' Palette (*c.* 3300 BC). From the early New Kingdom comes another hunting scene, painted on the side of an archery case. Not all hunting culminated in this mass killing, for there are representations of animals being captured alive for display, breeding or possibly taming.

Hunting in the marshes comprised fowling, fishing and possibly the killing of hippopotami. The pleasure with which these activities was regarded by the Egyptians is recorded in a very fragmentary papyrus entitled *The Pleasures of Fishing and Fowling*: 'A happy day when we go down to the marsh, that we may snare birds and catch many fishes in the two waters ... a happy day on which we give to everybody and the marsh goddess is propitious. We shall trap birds and shall light a brazier to Sobek.' The text was written by someone who was forced by his position to live away from the rural haunts which he used to frequent in his youth: 'Would that I were in the country always that I might do the things that were what my heart desired when the marsh was my town. . . .' The rest of this fragmentary text comprises enthusiastic descriptions of the huntsman's art, which provide an interesting supplement to set-piece scenes which survive in tombs. 'I settle at the ford and make ready for myself a screen after I have fastened my bait. I am in the cool breeze whilst my fishes are in the sun. I kill at every thrust, there is no stop for my spear. I make bundles of *bulti*-fish.' However, our keen fisherman has to admit 'gutting does not please me'. Having caught the fish, he hands over this messy job to a servant or to his poor wife. Many scenes depict this type of fishing. The fisherman lurks in the reeds on a papyrus raft and catches the fish with a harpoon-like spear. Hooks and nets were also available but these were mostly used by professional fishermen.

The papyrus goes on to describe the process of bird trapping:

I walk away from the river on the second day and the fifteenth day of the month and go down to the lake. Staves are on my shoulder, my poles and two and one-fifth cubits (of rope) under my arm. I attend to tugging at five cubits of draw rope by hand. The

75 The Hunters' Palette, from the predynastic period. Armed with bows and arrows and spears, the hunters encircle a variety of beasts, including lions, hyenas, antelope, a hare and a large ostrich-like bird. Length 66.5 cm (no. 20780).

76 Wooden archery case decorated with a hunting scene. Behind the huntsman are two bearers with dogs, an on the left is a schematic representation of nets used to trap creatures which had been driven into a wadi. Length 132.5 cm (no. 20648).

77 Fowling scene from the tomb of Nakht at Thebes. Hunting with throw-sticks was the sport of the well-to-do; professional hunters would use a net. At the front of the papyrus rafts were depicted a pet cat and a goose, both of which have been erased. These would have acted as retriever and decoy. Copy by Nina de Garis Davies.

water is sluggish. The thick cloth which the hand holds, we see it fall after we have heard the quacking of the pool's birds. We snare them in the net.

Another, more sporting way of catching birds is frequently depicted in tombs, such as that of Nakht. Nakht is shown with his family and servants on a light papyrus raft used for moving about in the shallow waters. It is made simply of papyrus reeds tied together, with a wooden platform in the centre on which to balance. In the left of the scene Nakht holds a bird by its feet. This is probably a stuffed decoy. In his other hand he holds the instrument of the kill, a throw-stick shaped like a snake, which acted in the same way as a boomerang, to break the bird's neck. His son prepares to hand him another. On the right-hand side of the scene he is shown having just cast his weapons, both the one in his hand and another given to him by his daughter. In the miraculous way of tomb paintings, both these

78 Old Kingdom relief showing a group of boys holding staves, perhaps taking part in a formation dance. One of them wears a lion mask. On the right, another group of boys are wrestling. Height 42 cm (no. 994).

throw-sticks have found their mark and two birds fall, their necks snapped.

Athletic games and sports were popular among the ancient Egyptians, whether practised informally or formally in the presence of the king or as part of religious ceremonies. Typical games included wrestling, boxing, 78 fighting with quarterstaves, ball games, gymnastics and acrobatics, and these are frequently shown as group activities.

Dance was also very popular in ancient Egypt, again in both religious and secular spheres. Rhythmic accompaniment was provided by clapping, cymbals, tambourines or chanting. Again, dancing was mainly a group 79 activity. Representations vary from slow, pos-

tured movement to lyrical, fluid or gymnastic performances.

Music in some form was an essential accompaniment to the dance, but it was also a recreational and religious art in its own right. Musical scenes are depicted from the Old Kingdom onwards. Although there were always musicians of both sexes, in the Old Kingdom men predominate while in the New Kingdom most of those shown are women. One theme that recurs again and again is that of the blind harper, usually male. The Egyptians seem to have lacked a written musical notation, so a blind performer would have been at no disadvantage. To gain some idea of the music played it is necessary to study the instruments, many of which survive. They can be divided into three categories – stringed, wind and percussion – and their range increased during the New Kingdom when new varieties were adopted from the Near East.

Stringed instruments comprised the harp, the lyre and the lute. Two varieties of harp are known. The arched, or bow, harp was used from the Sixth Dynasty onwards, but the angular harp appeared at the start of the New Kingdom, imported from Asia. The number of strings on these harps varies from four to ten and the size of the instruments is also variable. The strings were attached to the neck by pegs and to the sound box by a suspension rod, secured by a cord which could be adjusted to vary the tone. The harp was played by both men and women. The lute and the lyre both appeared from the Near East during the New Kingdom. The lute consisted of a long wooden neck attached to a sound box, which was

made either of wood or, in the case of small examples, a tortoise shell. A skin was stretched over the box for sounding and the neck had frets onto which the strings were pressed to make the notes. They were played with a plectrum. The lyre had two forms, asymmetrical and symmetrical, and consisted of two arms attached to a sound box. The two arms were joined by a yoke to which the strings were attached by cords, pieces of cloth or papyrus. Both these instruments were played mostly by women, either in orchestras or solo to accompany singers.

Various wind instruments are known, with and without reeds. The flutes of ancient Egypt were played obliquely. They could be made of reed or metal and came in different sizes. Reeded instruments were the clarinet and the oboe, which were played in pairs, one acting as a drone. The oboe tended to replace the clarinet in the New Kingdom and was mostly played by women. Trumpets were not used in orchestras, but only for military and religious purposes.

Of percussion instruments, those most commonly used in orchestras or for accompaniment were the tambourine and drum. Clappers, cymbals, bells and sistra were mostly reserved for religious uses.

The British Museum's collection contains several scenes showing musical groups. The first is of Old Kingdom date and shows a male 79 chamber group consisting of a harpist, a flautist and two singers. The New Kingdom scenes show a greater variety of instruments. One depicts a female ensemble at a banquet. 81 The group consists of a large lute, a clapping singer, a smaller lute, a double oboe and a tambourine or drum. A similar banquet scene from a Theban tomb shows a double oboe and three women clapping out a rhythm to accompany two dancers. The final scene depicts a 80 religious procession and indicates the pleasure to be had at a festival which would also have

79 Women performing a slow, mannered dance. They take short steps and raise their arms in the air. Two women clap out a rhythm. Above them is a male orchestra with a blind harpist, a flautist and two singers. Old Kingdom. Height of two registers 48 cm (no. 718).

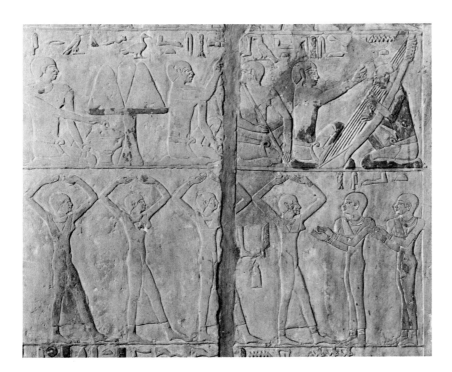

been a holiday. It represents a procession similar to one described by Herodotus, which took place at Bubastis – an occasion of great joy and frenzy. The worshippers went to Bubastis in barges, men and women packed in together: on the way some of the women kept up a continual clatter with castanets while some of the men played flutes. The rest sang and clapped their hands. Whenever they passed a town along the bank they brought the barge close inshore, making their music. The crowd in the barges yelled good-natured abuse at the women of the place, began to dance about or hitched up their robes to reveal their behinds. On reaching Bubastis they celebrated the festival with elaborate sacrifices and drank vast quantities of wine.

As already indicated, one of the main sources of employment for musicians was performing at banquets. Dinner parties seem to have been one of the favourite pastimes of the ancient Egyptian middle and upper classes, judging by the frequency with which they are depicted in tomb scenes. At the beginning of a feast the guests would be greeted by their hosts and offered flowered garlands by servants. They were also given scented cones for their hair, as described in the previous chapter. Guests did not sit round a large dining table as we do today but by small tables at which they

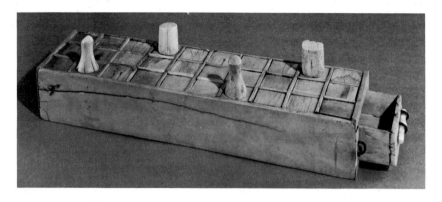

men and even women being sick into a bowl held by servants and being comforted by their neighbours as the jollity continues.

During a quiet evening at home there were other diversions to entertain the family. Adults could engage in a number of board games which were exceedingly popular amongst all walks of life. The most popular of these, called *senet*, began in the predynastic age and is even now played in Egypt in a recognisable form. The *senet* board was rectangular and divided into three rows of ten squares. The number of pieces allotted to each player could vary, but seven was usual. The game began by setting out the pieces alternately along the first fourteen squares. Movement was in a reversed S fashion, the object being to get all one's pieces off the board whilst preventing one's opponent from doing the same. If a piece was blocked it had to return to the start of the board.

Dice as we know them did not appear till the Graeco-Roman period, but the ancient Egyptians had alternative methods of moving the pieces. The first of these was a set of sticks, often shaped and marked like a human finger. One side of each stick was flat, the other rounded. The sticks were thrown down and the number of flat and round surfaces which landed uppermost were counted. In the modern form of the game the number of flat sides determines the throw and so it may have been in antiquity. The other form of dice was the astragalus, which was originally a knucklebone from a hooved animal, although the distinctive shape was soon copied in other materials. The face on which the astragalus fell again determined the throw.

Another popular game was called 'twenty squares', and is frequently found on the other side of a *senet* board. The markings were slightly different from those of *senet*. The middle of the three rows had twelve squares, while flanking it were two rows with four squares at

were served with food and wine. The hosts and honoured guests sat on chairs, while others sat on stools or cushions. In some scenes the men and women sit separately, while in others they mingle freely. This may represent the difference between married couples and single guests. The food and wine was heaped enticingly on stands and tables, almost like a buffet, although servants brought the food to the guests. During the meal musicians played and afterwards dancers, or possibly an acrobat, would perform. As the banquet continued, more and more wine was consumed, accompanied by such sentiments as 'Give me eighteen cups of wine, for I should love to drink to drunkenness, my inside is as dry as straw'. The end result of such indulgence is also recorded,

85 Children's toys: two balls made from vegetable fibre, two glazed composition tops and a wooden lion with a moving jaw operated by a piece of string.

one end and a long strip at the other: The players had five pieces each, which they placed in the empty strip. They began by moving the pieces up the four squares to the corner. The object of the game was to get the pieces safely down the centre row and off the board. As the opposing pieces moved in opposite directions, the tactic must have been to block and set back the advancing enemy. This game seems to have entered Egypt from the Near East. Other board games are known but the rules by which they were played are lost.

Meanwhile, the children could amuse themselves with a variety of toys. 85

Finally, we may count literature among the diversions of the ancient Egyptians. By no means all the Egyptians were literate, although a fair number probably were. These fortunates could read their favourite stories on papyrus rolls or on ostraca. For those who could not read, there was the storyteller, who would recount the tales of adventure and magic in which Egyptian literature abounds.

One of the most popular tales was the *Story of Sinuhe*, which is set during the Middle Kingdom. Sinuhe was a royal servant who, fearing for his life for a reason not named, fled Egypt and went to Palestine. After a great many adventures he was befriended by the local king who gave him land, a wife and command of the army. He led a long and prosperous life, occasionally fighting off jealous rivals, but in his old age he wished to return to his native land. His wish was granted by Pharaoh and so he returned to Egypt with great honour and was granted a fine house and an elaborate tomb with all the trimmings. Another travel tale, tinged with an element of magic, is that of the *Shipwrecked Sailor*. In this story are features which appear later in the *Odyssey* and the story of Sindbad the sailor. Like the *Odyssey*, it seems to belong to an oral tradition, and to have been part of a cycle of stories, as Sindbad is part of the *Thousand and One Nights*. Another group of stories in the *Thousand and One Nights* tradition is to be found in the Westcar Papyrus. This is a series of tales with a connecting narrative which provides the reason for telling the stories. The theme is again magic and the scene the court of Cheops, who is being entertained with tales of past wonders. He caps them all, however, by sending for a real magician who astounds the audience with his skill. Allegorical and moral tales were also popular, such as the *Blinding of Truth by Falsehood* and the *Tale of the Two Brothers*. A great many of these stories have been published in translation and make entertaining reading even today.

7 Popular Religion and Magic

Much is known and has been written about formal religion and cults in ancient Egypt, but the genuine beliefs of the average man are more difficult to identify. Lay people could not enter far into the major temples in order to worship; this was the prerogative of the priests who carried out the set rituals on behalf of the population. Nevertheless, religion played a vital part in the everyday life of the Egyptians, for they needed help against the hostile forces of nature which surrounded them and also against the machinations of their fellow men. Closely allied with religion at this level was magic, which was the practical means whereby men could combat these inimical powers.

Although the ordinary person was not allowed to take part in the daily ritual of the State gods, an opportunity for religious fervour came during the festivals or 'coming forth', when the statue of the deity was carried out in procession. The frenzy that attached itself to the festival of Bast at Bubastis in the Late Period has already been described. In a more serious vein were the mysteries of Osiris at Abydos. These represented the betrayal and murder of the god by his brother Seth, after which there were several days of mourning. Then followed a funeral procession of the statue of Osiris towards the traditional site of his tomb. At the site of the murder, the overthrow of Seth and his followers was re-enacted, after which Osiris was deemed to have risen again and his image was carried back to the temple amid the rejoicings of the crowd.

At Thebes there were two important festivals, belonging to the god Amun. The first of these was the festival of Opet, in which the statues of Amun, Mut and Khons were taken from their temples at Karnak to Luxor for a 'visit'. They proceeded by divine barque along the Nile, towed by the boats of the king and senior nobles. The procession was a great spectacle and the citizens of Thebes lined the bank for a rare vision of the god. This festival took place at the beginning of the year. Towards the end of the year the statue of Amun was carried across the Nile to the West Bank to visit the mortuary temples of the deceased kings, the ceremony culminating at the temple of Hatshepsut at Deir el-Bahri. The procession was eagerly followed by the citizens of the West Bank and was probably connected with the worship of dead ancestors in their funerary chapels.

The Egyptians may not have been able to worship the gods directly in their great temples, but they did have small, local shrines in which they could offer a prayer. A number of shrines to Amun are known to have existed on the West Bank, including one at Deir el-Medina. In that village there were also shrines to Hathor and to Ptah, patron of craftsmen, and other deities worshipped there were Thoth, Re-Harakhty, Khnum, Isis, Osiris and Anubis, as well as foreign gods such as Qadesh and Astarte. Also prominent was the cult of the local goddess Mertseger, who represented the great mountain of the West Bank known as El-Qurn. Evidence shows that the cult of this multitude of gods was organised by the villagers themselves, although they could no doubt have afforded to support a resident priesthood. This suggests that it was common practice in small communities for the inhabitants to act as their own priests, as a way of achieving closer contact with their gods.

The Deir el-Medina shrines were open for people to drop in to say their own prayers or make an offering. This commonly took the form of a votive stele showing the donor worshipping his chosen deity. Around the god a 86 number of ears were often depicted, to make quite sure that the prayer inscribed beneath was heard. These stelae, belonging to the Ramesside period, bear witness to a great upsurge of piety, or at least an increase in the

I am a man who swore falsely to Ptah, Lord of Truth, and he caused me to see darkness by day. I will declare his powers to those who know him and to those who do not know him, to the small and the great. Beware of Ptah, Lord of Truth. Behold! he does not overlook a person's deed.

Among the most popular cults at Deir el-Medina, and one which spread throughout the West Bank and later the whole of Egypt, was that of the deified Pharaoh Amenophis I and his mother Ahmes-Nefertari. The reason for the spread of his worship beyond his official mortuary temple was initially that he was the first ruler to be buried in the Valley of the Kings and had formed the group of artisans who were later to live at Deir el-Medina. He became the patron deity of the craftsmen and was seen as an intermediary between men and the gods. His main shrine was in the village, but there were at least five others scattered round the West Bank. Each of these had its own statue of the king, which differed slightly from the others in type and dress. These developed into different forms of the god, each with its own epithet, such as 'Amenophis of the Forecourt' and 'Amenophis Favourite (of Amun)'. Other deceased rulers were the object of similar cults in various locations, but none of them had the success of Amenophis I.

One of the main functions of the various forms of Amenophis I was the provision of oracles. In this he was not unique, for many gods provided oracular responses, but Amenophis I is one of the best attested and provides a good example of the procedures involved. The custom of seeking an oracle developed only in the New Kingdom, as part of the growing belief in a personal relationship with the gods, who, it was thought, might be willing to show an active interest in human affairs. The evidence indicates that most oracular responses were sought and received when the image of the god was carried out in procession. The statue of the deity was carried on the shoulders of

86 Stele from Memphis, dedicated to the god Ptah. On each side of the inscribed prayer are carved a number of ears to ensure that it would be heard. New Kingdom, *c.* 1200 BC. Height 21.5 cm (no. 1471).

open expression of personal belief, which had not previously been committed to writing. One explanation of this phenomenon may be that most of the evidence comes from Deir el-Medina, a community of exceptionally gifted, literate and comparatively well-off artisans, who were more capable and willing to express their beliefs than others at their level of society. On the other hand, Deir el-Medina has been thoroughly excavated, whereas the majority of other village and small town sites, which might yield similar evidence, have not.

The prayers on these stelae often take the form of a plea for mercy and recognition of the god's power over mankind for good or ill. Afflictions of the body, such as blindness, are frequently attributed to a god as punishment for some transgression against his might. Such a prayer was uttered by the workman Neferabu to the god Ptah:

specially purified laymen, while the priests walked alongside in attendance. In many cases the statue of the god was not visible but hidden in its shrine, although Amenophis I was carried openly for the people to see.

The applicant approached the god with his question, either spoken or offered in writing on papyrus or an ostracon. The range of questions varied enormously. Enquiries about health, job opportunities and absent relatives and friends were common. The god was also frequently asked to settle disputes, which more properly belonged in a court of law, but these instances may have been ones which a court was not able to settle. An example appears on an ostracon dating to the reign of Ramesses IV. A workman named Kenna had rebuilt for himself a ruined house, but when he had completed the work a certain Mersekhmet appeared and claimed that the god Amenophis had decreed that he was to share the house with Kenna, although he had had no part in the rebuilding. Kenna therefore presented his case to Amenophis via the scribe Horisheri and the god affirmed his claim to sole occupation of the dwelling.

The questions put to the oracle were usually phrased in a manner which required a simple yes or no answer. Alternatively, if seeking a guilty party in a crime, a list of names was read out until the god reacted to one of them. The method by which the god gave his response seems to have been that the men carrying the statue were forced by the will of the deity to move forwards or backwards, meaning yes and no respectively.

Another aspect of personal piety which is strongly attested at Deir el-Medina and which probably existed throughout Egypt was ancestor worship. It was the duty of the family to maintain the tombs of its relations, but there were also special festivals for the dead, such as the occasion when the statue of Amun visited the West Bank. Mortuary images were carried

in the procession of the god and later returned to the grave, where the family held a private feast. The purpose of these festivals was to renew the spirits of the deceased, so that they could appear again, like the sun god Re, every day. For this reason they are called the 'excellent spirits of Re'. Ancestor worship, however, did not cease at the tomb, for busts of departed 88 relations were kept in the home, in a niche in the main room of the house.

Rooms in the home contained a number of such niches, in which were kept not only the ancestral busts, but also images and stelae of the household deities. These could be any god with whom the inhabitants felt an affinity, but the general deities of the home were Bes and 89, 22 Taweret. Taweret, the pregnant hippopotamus goddess, was largely connected with fert-

87 Image of the god Amenophis I being carried in procession. The god would be greeted by a crowd wishing to ask his advice by oracle. Copy by Nina de Garis Davies.

88 Ancestral busts were placed in niches inside the home. They did not represent any particular ancestor, but those of the family generally. Height 24 cm (no. 61083).

89 The god Bes. His role was to bring happiness to the home, and he is often shown capering about, playing music and dancing. He also protected the house from the entry of evil, both by his grotesque appearance and by wielding a sword and shield. Height 49 cm (no. 61296).

ility and childbearing. Bes was a bandy-legged dwarf god with a wide mouth and protruding tongue. He was part lion, for his beard resembled a lion's mane and he had a lion's ears and tail. His role was to bring happiness to the home and to protect it from evil.

The power of Bes and Taweret in the household was amuletic and they frequently appear on small plaques and amulets which could be fastened to objects or worn about the person. This amuletic role takes us into the realms of magic, which the ancient Egyptians strongly believed in as a means of combating both the known and unknown forces of evil. A wide variety of amulets were available to protect the body from harm. Some reproduced hieroglyphic signs with abstract notions of power, such as life, strength, prosperity, stability and beauty, while many others took the form of deities. One of the most popular amulets was the *udjat*-eye of Horus. This was the eye knocked out by Seth and later returned and healed by Thoth. It was a symbol of light and was thought to ward off the evil eye.

Two further examples of interest are the cippi of Horus and magic wands made of hippopotamus ivory. The purpose of these two amulets was not to protect against unseen

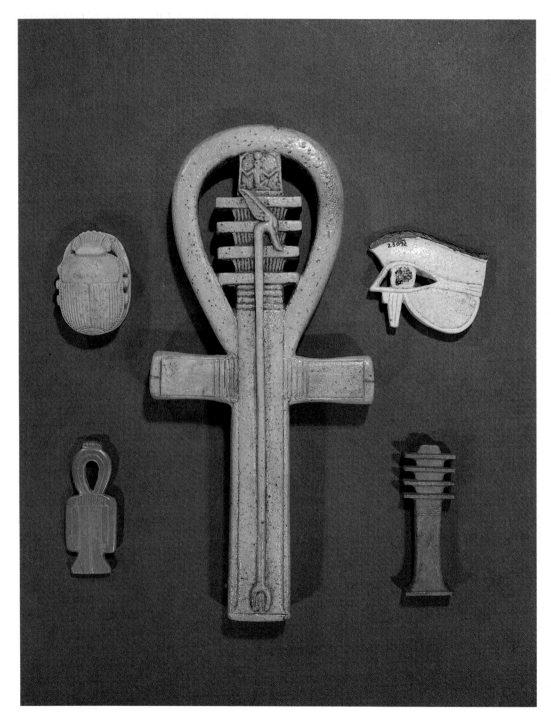

90 A collection of popular amulets. The sign of life (*ankh*) was commonly used as a decorative motif in conjunction with the *tjet* sign (bottom left), the protective amulet of Isis. Bottom right is the *udjat*-eye of Horus, which warned off the evil eye; and top left is the scarab beetle, another protective amulet.

91 A cippus of Horus. These small stelae were designed to protect the owner against harmful creatures. On the back are spells against snakes and scorpions, invoking the god Horus who had himself been stung by a scorpion and healed by his mother, Isis. Height 21 cm (no. 36250).

forces, but against the very tangible presence of animals and insects dangerous to man. The cippi of Horus take the form of stelae on which is depicted Horus the Child standing on two crocodiles and holding in his hands harmful creatures such as snakes, scorpions and lions, as well as an oryx gazelle, which was considered to have a baleful influence. Above Horus is a mask of the god Bes to provide additional protection.

The magic hippopotamus wands were designed to combat the approach of poisonous creatures such as snakes and scorpions during the night. They were laid near or under the bed and may have been used to draw magic circles round it before sleeping. Their power came partly from the material, hippopotamus ivory being considered very potent because of the strength of the animal from which it came.

A number of surviving magical texts on papyrus give us a good idea of how widely magic and superstition affected people's lives. Each day had attached to it magical significance which made it good, bad, partly good or partly bad. Calendars were drawn up showing the status of each day, so that people would know if it was safe to do certain things. The magical import of dreams as a means of divination was also taken seriously. *The Dream Book* gives a long list of dreams and their meanings, for example, 'If a man sees himself in a dream drinking warm beer: bad, it means suffering will come upon him. If a man sees himself in a dream carving up a female hippopotamus: good, it means a large meal from the palace.'

Another way in which magic affected the lives of the ancient Egyptians was in the sphere of medicine. In many ways Egyptian medicine was advanced for its time, especially in the case of observable ailments and wounds. A number of medical papyri exist in which there is a rational attempt to categorise diseases and which give an almost modern procedure for examination, treatments and

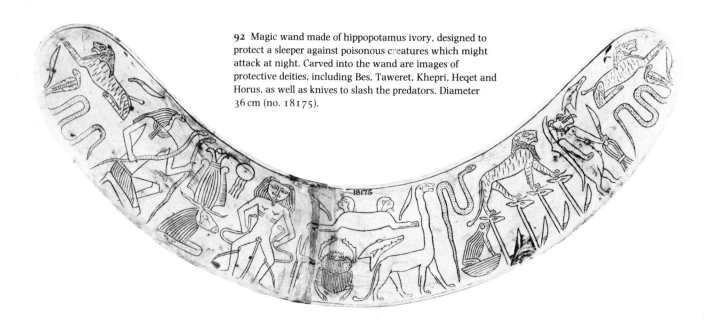

92 Magic wand made of hippopotamus ivory, designed to protect a sleeper against poisonous creatures which might attack at night. Carved into the wand are images of protective deities, including Bes, Taweret, Khepri, Heqet and Horus, as well as knives to slash the predators. Diameter 36 cm (no. 18175).

93 Part of a calendar listing the lucky and unlucky days of the year. Inauspicious days were marked in red, considered a malevolent colour (no. 10474, sheet 2).

prognosis. By trial and error the Egyptians learnt the use of many natural drugs and realised the importance of rest and care of the patient, as well as basic hygiene as a means of preventing the onset of certain problems. Nevertheless, there were many errors and great gaps in their knowledge of the human body and its workings. For instance, they realised that the heart was the centre of an elaborate series of vessels, but did not realise that it circulated only blood. It was believed that all the main systems of the body passed through the heart: blood, air, water, nerves and tendons. The Egyptians even thought that the stomach was connected to the heart and that many diseases were caused by an excess of food and its waste entering the circulatory system and polluting the body. The heart was also thought to be the seat of intelligence: the importance of the brain was not recognised, this organ being discarded as useless during the process of mummification.

Where science failed the medical men, magic took over. The power of suggestion may well have had some effect, but if all else had failed the recitation of a spell could be a source of comfort and hope to the sick. For this reason the medical profession included three groups of practitioners: surgeon-healers, priest-doctors and pure magicians. The nature of these healing spells can be gauged from an example designed to cure a complaint called 'half-head' (*gs-tp*) which is the origin of the Greek ἡμικρανία, in other words migraine:

A charm for exorcising headache. O Re, O Atum, O Shu, O Tefnut, O Geb, O Nut, O Anubis in front of the divine shrine, O Horus, O Seth, O Isis, O Nephthys, O Great Ennead, O Little Ennead, come and see your father concerning that enemy, dead man or dead woman, adversary male or female which is in the head of N born of M. To be recited over a crocodile of clay with grain in its mouth, and its eye of faience set in its head. One shall tie it and inscribe a drawing of the gods upon a strip of fine linen to be placed upon its head.

Thus protected by gods and charms, the ancient Egyptians were free to enjoy the bounties of their rich land.

The Dynasties of Egypt

Early Dynastic Period
(DYNASTIES I-II)
First Dynasty
c. 3100–2890 BC
Second Dynasty
c. 2890–2686 BC

Old Kingdom
(DYNASTIES III-VIII)
Third Dynasty
c. 2686–2613 BC
Fourth Dynasty
c. 2613–2494 BC
Fifth Dynasty
c. 2494–2345 BC
Sixth Dynasty
c. 2345–2181 BC
Seventh Dynasty
c. 2181–2173 BC
Eighth Dynasty
c. 2173–2160 BC

First Intermediate Period
(DYNASTIES IX-X)
Ninth Dynasty
c. 2160–2130 BC
Tenth Dynasty
c. 2130–2040 BC

Middle Kingdom
(DYNASTIES XI-XII)
Eleventh Dynasty
c. 2133–1991 BC
Twelfth Dynasty
c. 1991–1786 BC

Second Intermediate Period
(DYNASTIES XIII-XVII)
Thirteenth Dynasty
c. 1786–1633 BC
Fourteenth Dynasty
c. 1786–1603 BC
Fifteenth Dynasty
(Hyksos)
c. 1674–1567 BC
Sixteenth Dynasty
c. 1684–1567 BC
Seventeenth Dynasty
c. 1650–1567 BC

New Kingdom
(DYNASTIES XVIII-XX)
Eighteenth Dynasty
c. 1567–1320 BC
Nineteenth Dynasty
c. 1320–1200 BC
Twentieth Dynasty
c. 1200–1085 BC

Late Dynastic Period
(DYNASTIES XXI-XXX)
Twenty-first Dynasty
c. 1085–945 BC
Twenty-second Dynasty
c. 945–715 BC
Twenty-third Dynasty
c. 818–715 BC
Twenty-fourth Dynasty
c. 727–715 BC
Twenty-fifth Dynasty
c. 747–656 BC
Twenty-sixth Dynasty
664–525 BC
Twenty-seventh Dynasty
525–404 BC
Twenty-eighth Dynasty
404–399 BC
Twenty-ninth Dynasty
399–380 BC
Thirtieth Dynasty
380–343 BC

PERSIAN KINGS
343–332 BC

MACEDONIAN KINGS
332–305 BC

Graeco-Roman Period
after 305 BC
PTOLEMAIC KINGS
305–30 BC
ROMAN EMPERORS
after 30 BC

Short bibliography

C. Aldred, *The Egyptians*, 2nd ed. (London 1984)

J. Baines and J. Málek, *Atlas of Ancient Egypt* (London 1979)

M.L. Bierbrier, *The Tomb Builders of the Pharaohs* (London 1982)

E. Brovarski, S.K. Doll and R.E. Freed (eds), *Egypt's Golden Age* (Boston 1982)

J. Černý, *A Community of Workmen at Thebes in the Ramesside Era* (Cairo 1974)

J.R. Harris (ed.), *The Legacy of Egypt*, 2nd ed. (Oxford 1971)

W.C. Hayes, *The Scepter of Egypt*, 2 vols (New York 1953, 1959)

T.G.H. James, *An Introduction to Ancient Egypt* (London 1979)

T.G.H. James, *Pharaoh's People* (London 1984)

A. Lucas, *Ancient Egyptian Materials and Industries*, 4th ed., J.R. Harris ed. (Oxford 1962)

P. Montet, *Everyday Life in the Days of Ramesses the Great* (London 1958)

W.M.F. Petrie, *Objects of Daily Use* (Warminster 1974)

W.M.F. Petrie, *Tools and Weapons* (Warminster 1974)

Index

Photo acknowledgements

The photograph on pp. 2–3 is reproduced by kind permission of Mr T.G.H. James. Those in figs 1, 7, 38 and 46 are the copyright of the author. All other photographs have been provided by the Photographic Service of the British Museum, and the work of Peter Hayman is especially acknowledged. The line drawings in figs 2, 3, 4, 5, 6, 8, 9 and 47 are the work of Christine Barratt, Graphics Officer in the Department of Egyptian Antiquities.